ADA

Lovelace

first names

ADA
Lovelace

Ben Jeapes

Illustrations by Nick Ward

Abrams Books for Young Readers
NEW YORK

The facts in *First Names: Ada Lovelace* have been carefully checked
and are accurate to the best of our knowledge, but if you spot
something you think may be incorrect, please let us know.
Some of the passages in this book are actual quotes from Ada and other
important people. You'll be able to tell which ones they are by
the style of type: *I awoke one morning and found myself famous.*

Library of Congress Control Number 2019950354

ISBN 978-1-4197-4075-6

Text copyright © 2020 Ben Jeapes
Illustrations copyright © 2020 Nick Ward
Book design by Charice Silverman

2019 © as U.K. edition. First published in 2019
by David Fickling Books Limited

Printed and bound in U.S.A.
10 9 8 7 6 5 4 3 2 1

Abrams Books for Young Readers are available at special discounts when
purchased in quantity for premiums and promotions as well as fundraising
or educational use. Special editions can also be created to specification. For
details, contact specialsales@abramsbooks.com or the address below.

Abrams® is a registered trademark of Harry N. Abrams, Inc.

ABRAMS The Art of Books
195 Broadway, New York, NY 10007
abramsbooks.com

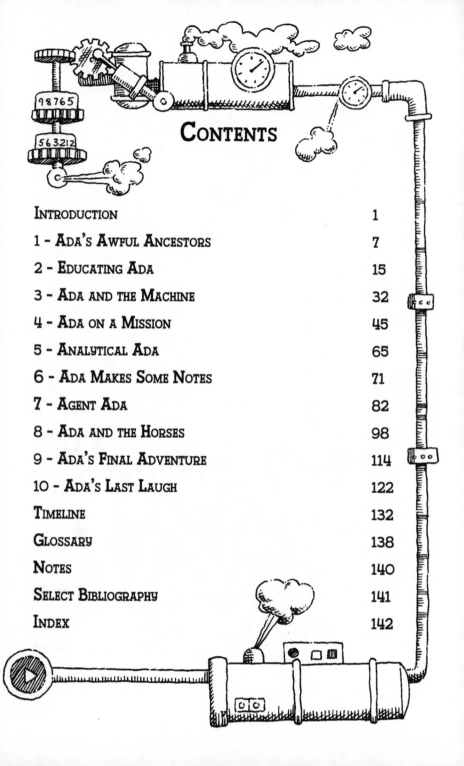

CONTENTS

INTRODUCTION

13 Piccadilly Terrace, London, January 15, 1816

It was a freezing cold January night when **a one-month-old baby was being stolen** from her father. A woman took the baby from the nursery.

It was the wrong century for electricity and central heating. The bedrooms of the five-floor mansion were snug and warm with coal fires, but the stairs and hallways were as dark and cold as the night outside. The thief crept away with her precious bundle, terrified of being discovered. In a house this size, it was a long way from the nursery to the front door—a lot of wooden floors and stairs, ready to creak a warning.

The stairs bent under every step the woman took. She held her breath each time she put a foot down, feeling the wood flex under her weight. But no sound came.

Silver moonlight splashed across the tiles of the front hall. There was one more challenge—the big, heavy front door, bolted shut against the night. She drew the bolts back one by one and **the metallic *clunks* echoed around the house**.

One, *clunk*.

It was like an explosion in her ears. She made herself keep going. If people woke up, they would be pouring down the stairs any minute now.

Two, *clunk*.

The woman grasped the door handle and pulled.

Cre-e-e-a-a-a-k . . .

Heart pounding, she stepped out into the night.

The streets were cold, dark and misty, but the city was already stirring, getting ready for the next day. It was very unusual for an upper-class lady to be out alone at this hour. **If she wasn't careful, she would attract attention.**

There was a carriage and a driver waiting for her. The woman hurried over and the driver helped her up. Once the door closed, she felt safer. He flicked the reins and the carriage lurched off.

The woman didn't relax until she reached her destination, a hundred miles away from London. But at least her plan worked. **She had successfully stolen her daughter** from her own home. The servants in the house would have obeyed her husband, the baby's father, and prevented her escape. A man's word was law, after all, and she knew they weren't completely safe.

In 1816, machines still ran on wind, steam, clockworks, or muscle power. Only a few scientists vaguely knew about electricity, and a "computer" was a person paid to do complicated sums—or computations—on paper.

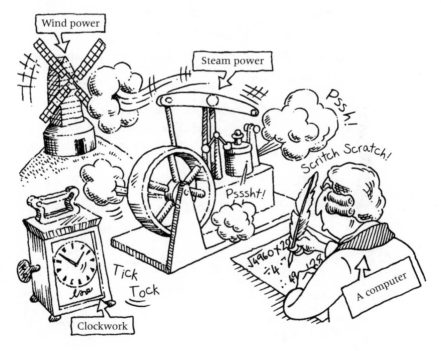

Wind power

Steam power

Pssh!

Scritch Scratch!

Psssht!

Tick Tock

Clockwork

A computer

This was the world the baby in the carriage was born into. Back then, machines were designed by men. Women in the nineteenth century had hardly any education and even less power. None of those male inventors would ever have imagined that, one day, one small machine might let you count and write, watch a movie, talk to friends, and more. But when the baby grew up, she wouldn't have been surprised at all.

One day, she would have a computer software language named after her, as well as a medal for people who have made great advances in the world of computers. **There's even a day named in her honor**, to celebrate women's achievements in science, technology, engineering, and math.

All in good time, though. At that moment, she was still only a month old!

Excuse me. Ada here. I'm the baby being stolen. The "thief" is my mother, Lady Annabella Byron, and she is not a common criminal!

Well, this was how your mother liked to tell the story . . .

Yes, but she believed she was saving me from my dreadful father, who gave an altogether different account of the event.

Hmm, your mom and dad were quite, erm, **interesting**, weren't they? Maybe we should start by talking about them . . . ?

Oh, my wretched family! Very well. Start a new chapter and tell everyone about them. But brace yourselves. It won't be pretty.

BYRON FAMILY TREE

William Byron
4th Lord Byron
Surprisingly little scandal

Murderer!

William Byron
5th Lord Byron
a.k.a. "The Wicked Lord"
Killed his cousin in an argument about grouse shooting. Spent all his money, so his son wouldn't inherit it.

Vice-Admiral John Byron
a.k.a. "Foul-Weather Jack"
Naval officer and adventurer. Almost started a war by claiming possession of the Falkland Islands, which the Spanish said belonged to them.

Oops!

You rascal!

William Byron MP
Racked up gambling debts and expected his dad to pay them. Ditched a rich bride to run off with his cousin. Then died before his dad, so the Byron title went to his cousin George.

Captain John Byron Gordon
a.k.a. "Mad Jack"
Blew all his money on wild living. Married two rich women and spent all their money. Had to take a new surname (Gordon) in one marriage deal. Left £22,000 debt ($44 million today) to his son George.

Just lend me a few thousand, Dad!

Lovely cash!

George Gordon Byron
6th Lord Byron
Violent temper. Abused drugs and alcohol. Debts forced him into marriage with a rich woman. Unfaithful husband (had girlfriends and boyfriends while he was married). World-famous poet.

Poetry is such agony.

Ada Byron

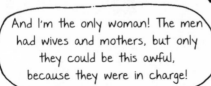

And I'm the only woman! The men had wives and mothers, but only they could be this awful, because they were in charge!

1   ADA'S AWFUL ANCESTORS

Ada's father, George Gordon, was the sixth Lord Byron (let's just call him Byron for short). He came from a long line of **drunkards, addicts, gamblers, and murderers**.

He carried on the family theme of wild, dangerous living, even though he didn't have any money before he got married! He liked to throw parties for his friends at the family home, Newstead Abbey in Nottinghamshire. Newstead had once been a monastery, and it's said Byron liked to drink his wine out of a cup made from an old skull found in the monks' graveyard. Ew! Byron started writing poetry at the age of fourteen, and in 1812, when he was twenty-four, he published the first half of his epic poem, *Childe Harold's Pilgrimage*—it sold out in just three days! **Byron became a superstar overnight.** In those days, he was about as cool as a YouTuber with fifty million followers. As he said himself: *I awoke one morning and found myself famous.*

Just think what he could have done if he'd written the whole poem!

Childe Harold made a small fortune for its publisher, but it didn't help Byron's debt problems. Strangely, he **wouldn't take any of the money** for himself.

My father loved being difficult. He believed only common people got paid, and he didn't want anyone to think he was common. I used to think the same thing, until I realized money is actually quite useful.

Byron's money troubles finally changed when he met Anne Isabella Milbanke.

HORRENDOUS HONEYMOON

Anne Isabella called herself Annabella. She was the cousin of a future prime minister and stood to inherit £20,000 (a few million dollars today) from a very old uncle. For Byron, it was the money that sealed the deal. In those days every penny a woman owned officially became her husband's when they got married—and then she had **absolutely no control over it**.

Byron might not want to earn money, but he had no problem with marrying a rich woman and taking all her wealth. It was a family tradition after all!

There was more to the match than just money, however. Byron and Annabella agreed about important things like social justice and helping people who were too poor to help themselves. His first speech in the House of Lords had been about workers in the north of England losing their jobs because of new fangled machines taking their places. **Byron was on the workers' side and so was Annabella.**

THE HOUSE OF LORDS

Britain's Parliament consists of the House of Commons and the House of Lords. Members of the Commons are elected, but to join the Lords, you just needed to *be* a lord. So, Byron was automatically a member. He did have to give a speech, though, and a member's first speech was usually on a subject very close to their heart.

They got married on January 2, 1815, had their first big argument on their honeymoon—it was downhill from then on. The unhappy couple moved to a fashionable part of London, and ten months later, on December 10, 1815, Ada was born. She was christened Augusta Ada Gordon, but generally addressed as Miss Byron. And to avoid confusion with her father's half-sister—also named Augusta—she was known by family and friends as Ada.

Byron cared about Ada—he even wrote a bit about her in the second part of *Childe Harold*, and by his standards that's probably the nicest thing he could have done.

But he wasn't ready to be tied down, and other things were going wrong too. Annabella's uncle had finally died, but then Byron learned, to his horror, that the old man's money would go to Annabella's mother first. **Byron wouldn't get a penny until she died.** By now Byron owed so much that debt collectors moved into his London home to make sure he didn't run off with any of the valuables.

The pressure of their money troubles made Byron so **angry and violent** that his personal servant had to be on constant guard to make sure he didn't attack his wife. Meanwhile, Annabella was worried that Byron was going mad—and she wasn't too pleased to discover that, despite being married, he was still having other relationships.

By January 15, 1816, Annabella had had enough. She was worried about her money and her own safety—and if she wasn't safe, then neither was her baby. That's why she ended up sneaking away from Byron, taking Ada with her.

MEANWHILE, BACK ON THE CARRIAGE . . .

Rattling as fast as it could toward Kirkby Hall, near Leicester—where Annabella's parents lived—the journey lasted days. Byron might have guessed where his wife was heading, but with no money, he couldn't afford to chase after her. However, the law was still on his side. If she was caught, she'd have to hand Ada back. So, when they stopped overnight to rest the horses, Annabella barely slept.

It was practically unheard of for a wife to leave her husband back then. **Annabella's reputation was at risk!** Even though Byron was a horrible husband, everyone would say *she* was the one in the wrong.

She wrote to a helpful doctor, who she hoped could prove Byron was mad. If he was mad, she reckoned, then he could be cured, and they could all get back to being one fairly unhappy family.

When they reached Kirkby Hall, Annabella could finally relax . . . a little. Her rich dad, Sir Ralph Milbanke, was there to protect her, while her anxious mom hurried off to London to find the best lawyer she could.

When Annabella got the doctor's report, it said there was nothing wrong with Byron: he wasn't mad, he was just bad. There was no hope for their marriage now, because **Byron would never change**.

Bad, not mad? How very disappointing.

By that time, however, Annabella had found herself a way out of the relationship that would protect her own reputation. One of Byron's old girlfriends had revealed a secret about Byron SO SCANDALOUS, that we can't even tell you what it was. Annabella threatened to spread the secret around unless Byron stayed away.

He didn't argue.

SCANDAL!

And What About Ada?

Baby Ada enjoyed living with her grandparents. It was nice being with grown-ups who didn't argue all the time. She ate, she slept, she grew . . . Then, in April 1816, when Ada was three months old, Annabella received the best possible news. **Byron had fled to Europe!** In those days, if you owed money, you could be sent to jail, even if you were a lord. Too many people in England wanted Byron arrested, so he'd quickly made plans to leave the country.

And he'd fled in style. Somehow persuading the bailiffs to look the other way, Byron had sold off just about everything he owned, for whatever he could get. He'd written to Annabella, enclosing a ring for Ada, and then he'd traveled to Dover in a fancy carriage just like one the French Emperor Napoleon owned. It would have cost $600,000 today—if Byron had actually paid for it, which of course he hadn't!

2   EDUCATING ADA

Little Ada quickly settled into life at Kirkby Hall. It was a big, exciting house and she loved to toddle around its huge rooms and corridors and galleries.

She had no idea that her grandmother slept with loaded pistols by her bed, or that burly servants patrolled the grounds to **fight off any potential kidnappers**. Byron might be gone, but the law was still on his side; he could change his mind and come home one day to reclaim Ada.

So Ada didn't get out much. But it wasn't just because of security. Privacy mattered too. Ada was a celebrity baby. Since her famous parents had separated, everyone wanted a glimpse of her.

Then, when Ada was eight, **Byron died** in Greece.

Being a celebrity, his death made headlines around the world. Everyone remembered where they were when they'd heard the news. Even people who had never met Byron were beside themselves. When his body was brought back to England for the funeral, the streets were lined with mourners.

Ada cried about his death when she was told, but she wasn't sure why. Annabella assumed that since Ada couldn't possibly remember her father, she must be upset because her mother was now a widow. Ada must be crying for her.

Ada might have cried more if she had realized what her father's death meant for her own childhood.

The good thing was that money stopped being a problem. With her husband dead, Annabella could take care of her own cash again and spend it very, *very* carefully. She owned properties in London and around the country, which made her extremely rich.

And Annabella could now bring Ada up exactly how she wanted, which wasn't great for Ada. Even while Byron was abroad, Annabella had been forced to educate Ada however he had wanted. Not anymore. Now Annabella's greatest priority was to make sure Ada **didn't take after her dad**—in any way.

So Annabella **banned poetry** from the house. There were no fairy tales or bedtime stories either. Nothing to inspire the imagination. If something wasn't absolutely true, then Ada didn't need to know about it.

No Friends

Ada grew up a lonely girl. Annabella didn't let her play with the village children because they might tell her stories and spark her imagination! In any case, as far as Annabella could see, children were just small adults, so she decided Ada could hang out with carefully chosen grown-ups instead—serious, unpoetic ones.

Upper-class girls like Ada didn't go to school—school came to them! Annabella hired a whole range of tutors in "suitable" subjects: Latin, chemistry, French, music (Ada loved playing the harp), math, and shorthand (a system of symbols that make it possible to write really quickly). Ada was expected to take notes on everything she read, and because she read so much, shorthand was a speedy way of getting it all down.

To make sure Ada concentrated on her schoolwork —and didn't sneak off to write poetry instead— Annabella invented a ticket system. If Ada did well, she got tickets that she could use to buy things Annabella approved of, like books (as long as she chose the right ones).

Absolutely forbidden

W. & J. Grimm
Children's and Household Tales
Collected Sonnets
W. Shakespeare
W. Wordsworth and Coleridge
Lyrical Ballads, with a Few Other Poems
The Rime of the Ancient Mariner
Samuel Taylor Coleridge

Useful Knowledge: A Familiar and Explanatory Account of the Various Productions of Nature, Mineral, Vegetable and Animal
W. Bingley
The Dictionary of Arts, Sciences and Literature
A Book of Geometry

Suitable reading for Ada

Byron
Childe Harold's Pilgrimage

If Ada did badly, tickets were taken away. If she was careless with her math problems, or didn't pay attention in lessons, there was a two-ticket fine. Then, if Ada ran out of tickets, **she had to stay in a cupboard** until Annabella thought she seemed ready to work again.

In the nineteenth-century, young ladies were also expected to be able to walk and stand in exactly the right way. These were important skills for attracting a future husband. Annabella worried that Ada wasn't doing it right. So, from the tender age of five, Ada had to **lie on a drawing board** for hours on end.

It was very uncomfortable and distracting.

AND WHAT ABOUT DAD?

A few weeks after Byron's body was brought back to England and buried, Annabella took Ada to visit the ship that had carried him home. To Ada it just seemed like a big, empty boat. She didn't even know what her father had looked like. How could she? There were no computers, no cameras.

Strangely, there actually was a **portrait of Byron** hanging in the house, though Annabella had hidden it behind a green curtain. She worried her daughter would react badly if she saw it.

Ada did ask to look at it, when she was little . . .

Noooo! Not even a peek until you are married, young lady!

Are you surprised that I learned to be a little afraid of my mother?

She didn't ask again.

IMAGINATION ALERT!

In 1826, when Ada was ten, her mom took her on a year-long vacation to Europe. They traveled around Switzerland and Germany and Italy, as rich people often did in those days.

Of course, there was a risk that the vacation might spark Ada's imagination, but Annabella thought it a risk worth taking. In any case, she would be with Ada every step of the way. What could possibly go wrong?

Annabella may have forgotten that in 1816, soon after he fled England, Byron had stayed in Switzerland. He'd thrown a house party on the shores of Lake Geneva for a bunch of writer friends and they'd organized a mini-competition to see who could write the best horror story. The winning story was written by an eighteen-year-old named Mary Shelley—it was called *Frankenstein*.

If there was something in the Swiss air that encouraged writers, it certainly got to Ada, because when they got home, she started writing stories too.

Once upon a time, a princess and two ladies were on vacation in the mountains . . .

None of Ada's stories would become as famous as *Frankenstein*, but it was clear **she did have an imagination**, and one day it would make her one of the most famous women of her time—but for a completely different reason.

Naturally, Annabella was not pleased that her daughter was showing signs of being creative. Something had to be done!

MATH, MORALS, AND MINDS

Annabella had her devoted doctor, Dr. King, examine Ada. He came up with a theory that Ada had "moral incontinence."

Incontinence usually means that you can't control going to the bathroom. But "*moral* incontinence," according to Dr. King, meant that Ada couldn't control her wild, random thoughts or her imagination.

There was a cure, Ada's mom was relieved to hear: it was math! **Lots and lots of math**. So, while other children learned "Twinkle, Twinkle Little Star," Ada had to memorize complicated mathematical equations.

In those days, it was quite fashionable for women to take an interest in math—up to a point. It seemed obvious to male mathematicians that women would never be able to work stuff out for themselves. Some people believed that because men's bodies were usually stronger than women's, they must have stronger minds too. So if a woman over-exercised her mind, the consequences could be disastrous!

Ada proved those mathematical men completely wrong. **She absolutely loved learning**—and she was very good at it. By the time she was twelve, she had knowledge and ideas way beyond most other twelve-year-olds, then or now. Ada believed Annabella's warnings about ending up like her father, and she desperately wanted to be sane and normal, so she threw herself into mathematics to prevent "moral incontinence," but also because:

I was desperate to know all sorts of things! Why is a rainbow always curved? Why don't planets fly off into space? And to find those answers, I needed to know math.

Annabella never realized that to be really good at math, you need a *really good* imagination. Writers and poets use words to tell stories. To Ada, mathematical symbols were like a language, which could tell a different sort of story. Putting math and imagination together she came up with an amazing idea . . .

ADA SPREADS HER WINGS

Crunch. Snap. Squelch.

And other disgusting noises that you really don't want to hear coming from under your bed. Especially when you're lying on it.

Ada was twelve years old and her cat, Puff, was eating a bird. She laid there for a while and listened to the sounds of crunching bones. Poor bird. She pictured the beautiful creature—alive—in her mind's eye. Sleek and feathered, it was perfectly designed for flight. (She tried not to think about what was happening under her bed.)

$$\text{Lift} = C^L \times (1/2 \rho V^2) \times A$$
$$\text{Drag} = C^D \times (1/2 \rho V^2) \times A$$

SQUELCH! CRUNCH!

Hmm. A human can flap their arms up and down and they'll just get tired arms. A bird gives a wave of its wings and up it goes.

The year was 1828, and by then scientists knew roughly how wings worked. They just didn't know how to make a machine that would move fast enough for the air to lift it off the ground. They did know that getting off the ground needed quite complicated math. Get that right, and **anyone could fly**. Even Ada. In theory.

Ada found herself carried away by the idea. She started to study the bodies of dead birds, especially their wings, to work out how they did it.

She studied their bones and muscles too, trying to understand how the whole body of a bird helps it fly.

She decided to call her new science of how to fly . . . "flyology" and she planned to write a book about it!

Ada **tricked out a room with ropes and pulleys**, to help practice moving through the air. She drew up plans for a flying machine that could be used to deliver mail. That way, the mailman could travel in straight lines (much faster) and avoid annoying obstacles like mountains and rivers that slowed him down.

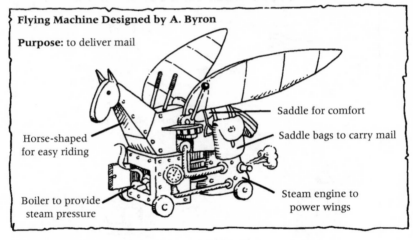

Flying Machine Designed by A. Byron

Purpose: to deliver mail

Saddle for comfort

Saddle bags to carry mail

Horse-shaped for easy riding

Boiler to provide steam pressure

Steam engine to power wings

MEASLES. PHEW!

Flyology was Ada's first real attempt to combine science and imagination, and it kept her busy for most of 1828. She also kept up her normal studies and started to work on a planetarium—a map of the night sky—showing the nearest planets to Earth and a lot of the major stars.

Then in 1829, when Ada was thirteen, **she fell ill**. She'd been getting terrible headaches since the age of seven. Now she had a really bad case of measles.

Today, measles can be prevented by a simple vaccination, but that wasn't available in the nineteenth century. Measles was much more common then, and it was often deadly. Ada's measles kept her practically paralyzed and **in bed for the next three years**! At sixteen, she was still walking with crutches, and she was plagued with aches, pains, and "nervous attacks" for the rest of her life.

Who knows, if she'd kept at flyology, Ada might have made a discovery that could have made flight work. But by the time she was better, she'd realized that the right technology just didn't exist yet. She stopped working on her flyology book and stopped writing stories, and as she started getting better, her mom breathed a sigh of relief.

ARGUING ADA

Meanwhile, the relationship between mother and daughter was still a stormy one, especially since Annabella had brought in some friends—three unmarried women—to keep an eye on Ada. **Ada nicknamed them "the Furies,"** because in Greek mythology, the Furies are spiteful goddesses of vengeance. (Ada *was* allowed to read Greek myths, because they were considered essential for a good education in those days.)

The name was a perfect fit for Ada's real-life Furies, who hated her about as much as she hated them. They would exaggerate stories about Ada, to get her into trouble. Annabella always believed the Furies and **never listened to Ada's version of events**.

Ada was really starting to get on her mother's nerves. Sometimes she refused to sleep in her bed (especially once she was over the measles) or fussed about her food. Annabella complained that she turned every disagreement into "a French Revolution." And often, Ada argued with her mom *by letter*—even though they lived in the same house! (Of course, she couldn't argue by text, like today's teenagers—and she had no idea that the work she would later become famous for would help make texting possible.)

Ada's letters were always very long and very logical, so Annabella only had herself to blame. She had wanted Ada to be logical after all. And, as she got older, Ada was certainly unusual, but she wasn't mad. She wasn't poetic. **She wasn't like Byron**. Success!

Great Britain in the early nineteenth century was a very difficult place *not* to be imaginative in. Amazing things were happening.

We have factories driven by a new wonder power source called steam!

CLACK! CLATTER! CLACK! PSsst!

Steam power meant people can travel a hundred miles in just a few hours. When my father was alive it could take days by horse and carriage.

They built a National Gallery of Practical Science in London to show off all the new inventions as they came out.

Gas mask

Pocket thermometer

I'm so looking forward to visiting. It seems there is something new nearly every week.

ALL CHANGE!

People were better informed than ever about all sorts of things. The London Zoo had opened, so for the first time ever, ordinary people could see some of **the most amazing animals in the world**—zebras, kangaroos, emus,

Why does that horse have such a long neck?

elephants, and giraffes—with their own eyes.

In the mid-1800s, for the first time, more people lived in cities than in the countryside—which brought new problems of poverty and hygiene. The government was just starting to take this seriously, with new laws.

In short, Ada was living in a country that was changing, and she saw that change could be a good thing. It wasn't something to be afraid of. Technology, she realized, could be helpful in every area of life.

And Ada was changing too, from a child to an adult. For a young lady of Ada's status, the most important thing was to carry on the family name—by **finding a spouse and having children**.

"The Season" was the name for a series of parties and events for people of the right social class. It was designed to make finding a husband or wife much easier. For a young woman, it began when she was presented to the king and queen.

Not all young ladies were eligible. They had to be of good character and nominated by someone who had been presented themselves (as Annabella had been, years before). After the presentation, they were officially grown-up and on the marriage market.

Yes, sooner or later, no matter how much she loved equations and inventing flying machines . . .

3   ADA AND THE MACHINE

On a hot day in May 1833, Ada—now seventeen—waited with a hundred other girls in a side room of the palace. Music and laughter drifted in through the doors.

Outside, in the main ballroom, His Majesty King William IV, and his wife Queen Adelaide, were entertaining **a hundred rich young men** on the lookout for wives.

Each of the girls looked and felt like a princess.

Well, maybe there was one who didn't.

At long last the doors opened, and the girls walked slowly toward the head of the ballroom, where the royal couple sat. As each girl approached Their Majesties, an usher announced her name. Finally Ada's name was called and she stepped forward. A soft murmur rippled around the room. Ada was used to this. She had been a celebrity her whole life, and people still wanted to catch a glimpse of Lord Byron's daughter.

Ada curtseyed, then backed away to make room for the next young lady. You were expected not to turn your back on the king. And that was it. The king officially knew that she existed, so from then on Ada would be on the guest list for London parties and balls throughout the Season. And she'd be expected to find herself a husband at one of them, because that was what young ladies did.

But Ada was still only seventeen. She had other plans. She wanted to make her mark in this changing world. She just needed to find a way . . .

It just so happened that Ada's math tutor, Mary Somerville, had invited her to a party, and on June 5, 1833, Ada met the man who would become **her best friend for life**.

Not Really Husband Material

Ada noticed him immediately. He definitely wasn't husband material, but maybe that's why she liked him. He was rich, famous, and probably the most logical person she would ever meet:

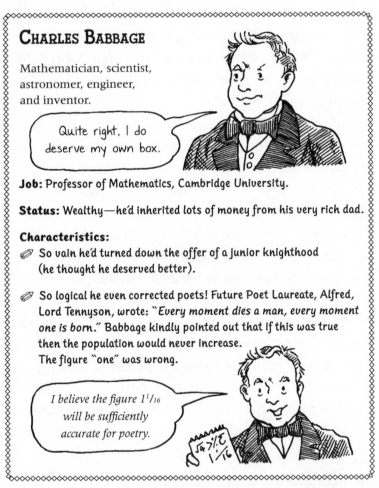

CHARLES BABBAGE

Mathematician, scientist, astronomer, engineer, and inventor.

> Quite right, I do deserve my own box.

Job: Professor of Mathematics, Cambridge University.

Status: Wealthy—he'd inherited lots of money from his very rich dad.

Characteristics:

- So vain he'd turned down the offer of a junior knighthood (he thought he deserved better).

- So logical he even corrected poets! Future Poet Laureate, Alfred, Lord Tennyson, wrote: "*Every moment dies a man, every moment one is born.*" Babbage kindly pointed out that if this was true then the population would never increase.
  The figure "one" was wrong.

> *I believe the figure $1^1/_{16}$ will be sufficiently accurate for poetry.*

Even though **Ada was seventeen and Babbage was forty-two**, they hit it off right away. They seemed to really understand each other.

Babbage liked to hold parties himself, for rich and famous guests, but not the sort with dancing and music and games. There was tea, but no cake, only brown bread and butter. Also, you didn't go to Babbage's parties to have fun; you went to be interesting and interested.

Babbage was very picky about his guests. They had to have at least one of three things: intellect, beauty, or rank. Ada certainly passed that test—she had all three. **She was top of the list** for his next party, on June 17.

Ada couldn't wait. She'd heard about Babbage's little gatherings and knew exactly what to expect: they had nothing to do with husband hunting.

BABBAGE'S BASH

Ada felt a tingle of excitement as she moved through the crowd on that warm June evening. She was accompanied by Annabella, and surrounded by some of the best-known names in the British Empire. Writers, explorers, and politicians. Soldiers, sailors, and scientists. But Ada, Babbage, and the other guests all had different ideas about what was the most interesting thing at the party.

For some of the guests, it was Ada herself. They just wanted to see the famous Lord Byron's daughter. Others wanted to examine one of Babbage's little machines. He was a great tinkerer. His latest device was a little mechanical dancer made of silver that he'd rescued from a junk shop and restored to full working order.

The movement of the dancing figure was so beautiful, so lifelike, that Babbage found it hard to shift people's attention to the real attraction. His baby—and the thing Ada had come to see, was a much, much cleverer machine that he had designed himself. Babbage kept it in a dust-free room next door. Only Ada found this the most interesting thing at the party. It might not look as beautiful as the dancer, but it actually served a purpose. She didn't know it at the time, but **this machine was going to change her life**.

It was a mass of metal wheels and cogs, more complex than any clock. This was Difference Engine No. 1 and, at the time, it was **the most remarkable machine in the world**.

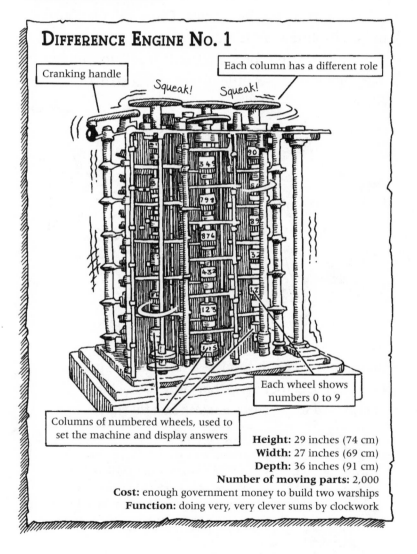

DIFFERENCE ENGINE No. 1

Cranking handle

Each column has a different role

Squeak! Squeak!

Each wheel shows numbers 0 to 9

Columns of numbered wheels, used to set the machine and display answers

Height: 29 inches (74 cm)
Width: 27 inches (69 cm)
Depth: 36 inches (91 cm)
Number of moving parts: 2,000
Cost: enough government money to build two warships
Function: doing very, very clever sums by clockwork

THE BEAUTIFUL MACHINE

Machines and buildings were getting bigger and better, so engineers needed more and more complicated calculations to get them right. Those calculations had to be absolutely accurate, on first try. When it came to building a ship or a bridge, if just one number in a calculation was a little bit wrong, a structure could collapse.

Maximum load 3000 tons

Maximum load 300 tons

You copied the figures wrong!

This is where the Difference Engine came in. A human would get a few calculations right, but as the pressure increased, sooner or later they'd make a mistake. Babbage believed that only a machine could be **guaranteed to get every answer exactly right**.

Some people thought the Difference Engine was just a fancy calculator, but it was much cleverer than that. The trouble was, before **it** could work out the complicated calculations, **you** had to do some simple calculations first.

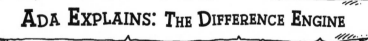

ADA EXPLAINS: THE DIFFERENCE ENGINE

I've started by cubing some numbers. For example, three cubed is 3 x 3 x 3 = 27

I've worked out the first few cubes and I've set the wheels of the Difference Engine to show the answers.

The first three cubes:
1 x 1 x 1 = 1
2 x 2 x 2 = 8
3 x 3 x 3 = 27

When the handle is turned, the wheels outside and inside begin to spin

Rows of wheels change to reveal the answers

Wheels and levers carry the numbers through the machine

The Difference Engine looked at the differences between the human's answers (hence the name) and worked out the calculation that produced them, all by clockwork. Then, it could use the same calculation to work out bigger and bigger numbers.

So, the only limit is the number of wheels—and the operator's ability to do simple math!

However, Difference Engine No. 1 was just a demonstration model, a smaller version of a much larger design Babbage was supposed to be working on. The new machine would be steam-powered, clockwork, and able to handle even bigger numbers.

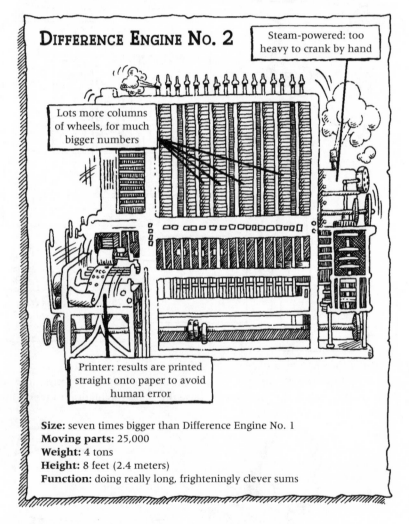

DIFFERENCE ENGINE No. 2

Steam-powered: too heavy to crank by hand

Lots more columns of wheels, for much bigger numbers

Printer: results are printed straight onto paper to avoid human error

Size: seven times bigger than Difference Engine No. 1
Moving parts: 25,000
Weight: 4 tons
Height: 8 feet (2.4 meters)
Function: doing really long, frighteningly clever sums

The British government was taking Babbage's idea very seriously. They had already given him **a massive amount of money** for research—enough to build two warships—but Babbage had spent most of that developing Difference Engine No. 1. Meanwhile, the government was kind of hoping he would actually produce Difference Engine No. 2 any day now.

Unfortunately, Babbage had the same problems as many geniuses:

- He was a perfectionist. Playing around with the idea, tinkering with it, making it absolutely right, was far more interesting than actually finishing the job.

- Babbage liked to be the boss, and his social skills weren't great. His chief engineer on the Difference Engine was a brilliant designer called Joseph Clement. One reason they stopped working together was because Babbage treated him like, well, a servant.

Milk and two sugars, please.

One of the best engineering minds in the country

✏️ If Babbage could understand something, he couldn't for the life of him see why everyone else didn't.

Some of the best minds in the country

But, Mr Babbage, how exactly does it work?

I'm very glad you asked that! *Whatever number is found upon the column of first differences will be added to the number found upon the table column. The same first difference remaining upon its own column, the number found upon the column of second differences will be added to that first difference . . .*

Ada was only seventeen, but she understood Babbage, and she understood the Difference Engine. She could have explained it much better than Babbage did—if anyone had asked.

No one at Babbage's party—apart from Babbage himself—would have taken her seriously if she'd spoken her thoughts out loud, but she immediately knew that **this machine was the future**. It made so many things possible.

Ada didn't know exactly what the future held, but from that moment on, she definitely wanted to be part of it. Finally, **she knew what she wanted to do with her life**. She had always enjoyed studying math anyway.

4 ADA ON A MISSION

Now Ada knew where she was heading, she needed to work on her math skills—she was nowhere near the world-class level of Babbage. So, she made sure she had the very **best math tutors around**, even though aristocratic ladies weren't supposed to bother themselves with such a complex subject. Ada's tutor Mary was a lady, and she was brilliant at math; she just wasn't wealthy enough to be aristocratic.

MARY SOMERVILLE
1780-1872

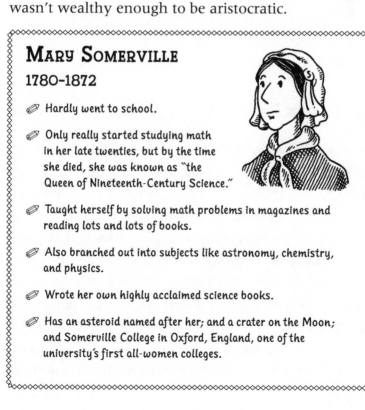

- Hardly went to school.

- Only really started studying math in her late twenties, but by the time she died, she was known as "the Queen of Nineteenth-Century Science."

- Taught herself by solving math problems in magazines and reading lots and lots of books.

- Also branched out into subjects like astronomy, chemistry, and physics.

- Wrote her own highly acclaimed science books.

- Has an asteroid named after her; and a crater on the Moon; and Somerville College in Oxford, England, one of the university's first all-women colleges.

Other tutors could only teach her by letter, which was a bit like virtual learning but much, much slower. Mary, however, was able to tutor Ada in person.

While she was studying, Ada kept in touch with Babbage and followed all the news about the Difference Engine, much like people today might follow a celebrity vlogger. Only, as with her tutors, it all had to be done by letter or from articles in newspapers rather than instantly, on a screen. She pestered Babbage for plans and diagrams so that she could keep up with everything he was doing.

This kept Ada busy enough to put off finding a husband for a couple more years.

All Change Up North

Meanwhile, Annabella tried to keep Ada busy with other things. In 1834, she took her on a tour of towns and cities in the north of England and the Midlands, where the Industrial Revolution was in full swing. Areas that had been farmland 100 years earlier were now **totally transformed** by industry. Factories and mills had sprung up, thanks to new steam-powered technology, and they churned out textiles and made machines that were sold worldwide.

This was a really exciting time to be alive . . . if you had money. Once upon a time, most things had been made in small workshops or at home by hand, but now **machines in factories were taking over**. Businesses got rich because they could make more goods and pay fewer people (and the government benefited by collecting taxes from them).

The workers who kept their jobs weren't paid much, and many now had no work at all. If you wanted a job—even a low-paid one—you had to go to cities, like Birmingham and Manchester, which were becoming huge.

Annabella cared deeply about social justice, and she hoped that by taking Ada to see these factories for herself, her daughter would care too. But, aside from getting away from the Furies, Ada was most interested in the **scientific developments**. She found a visit to a cloth factory in Coventry especially interesting.

A Code in the Card

The factory was hot, crowded, and noisy. It was packed to the rafters with fast-moving machinery, and men, women, and children working twelve or more hours a day.

Ada and Annabella worked their way through the rows of spinning machinery, carefully pulling their wide skirts out of reach of whirling cogs and levers. One slip in a place like this could be lethal—limbs often ended up mangled or even lopped off altogether.

The foreman demonstrated one of the latest looms and the two women watched with amazement as the machine wove a complicated pattern onto a piece of cloth, all by itself! He handed each of them a slim rectangle of tough cardboard, with rows of holes punched into it. It looked like there was some kind of pattern or code in the holes, but it was impossible to tell what.

Ada's heart pounded with excitement. This was a Jacquard card. She had in her hands an example of **the first ever machine-readable technology**! Babbage had told her about them—they could make a machine *think* for itself. She hadn't understood what he meant before, but now it all fell into place.

This is a Jacquard card. Doesn't look like much does it? But here's what it can do . . .

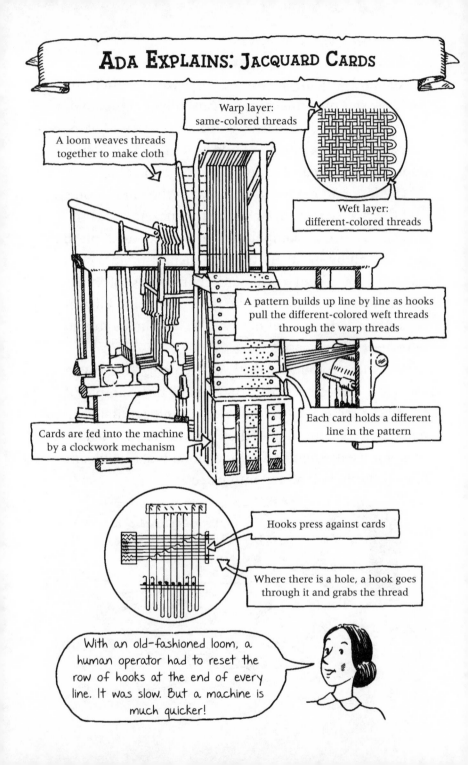

A Husband for Ada

Back home again, Annabella's search for a husband for Ada began in earnest. Thanks to the family name, the suitors weren't exactly rushing in—no one was in a hurry to marry the daughter of Lord Byron.

Some people thought Ada was "a beauty," but Ada herself didn't agree, and she certainly didn't act like one. She once commented that her jaw looked big enough to write the word "mathematics' on, and she dressed so plainly that one friend joked **it was hard to tell her apart from the servants**.

But Annabella was determined. She was still trying to live down the disgrace of her own marriage and she really wanted Ada to settle down with a nice, normal husband, and have lots of children.

In desperation, she even considered Babbage. He wasn't a lord, but he was rich and respectable—which was the next best thing—and the pair were already friends. On the other hand, he was old enough to be

Ada's father, he already had children, and he really wasn't interested.

Ada finally changed her mind about finding a husband when she realized that marriage could have one big plus. Until the day of her wedding, Ada had to live with her mother and **put up with her mother's awful friends**. Yes, at age nineteen, the frightful Furies were still plaguing her.

So, Ada was in a fairly receptive mood when Mary Somerville's son, Woronzow (his dad was Russian), introduced her to his friend from college, Lord William King.

William was a scientist too, interested in agriculture, and a Fellow of the Royal Society (i.e., very clever!). He was shy, and enjoyed Ada's company. He wasn't bothered by the Byron connection and happily let her continue studying math.

Ada came with £16,000 (about $1.3 million today) of Byron's money, and £14,000 (about $1.1 million today) of Annabella's and she stood to inherit her mom's money too when her mom died. She was bright, chatty, and always fun to be with.

William was actually quite a catch. There was a big age difference—he was thirty and Ada was nineteen—but neither of them minded. They met in the spring of 1835 and got married in July. To Annabella's delight, the Honorable Miss Ada Byron became Lady Ada King.

Lords and ladies, like Ada and William, usually married for money and status first. Love came second—if you were lucky.

William would now have control of all Ada's money, but he would give her £300 (about $25,000 today) a year. Not much if you have to live off it, but not bad at all if you're married to a rich lord who pays for everything else.

The new Lord and Lady King spent their honeymoon at William's favorite house (he owned several), Ashley Combe in Somerset.

ADA PASSES A TEST

Annabella was delighted with the match, but now came the ultimate test. Annabella had agreed, once Ada was married, that she would send her daughter all the things that Byron had left her. This included the ring he had sent the day he fled the country, an inkstand, some other trinkets, and a large, flat, square package.

Annabella was so anxious about this last item that she made sure her favorite doctor, Dr. King (no relation to William), was "just visiting" when Ada opened it.

Ada probably guessed it was the painting that had hung behind a curtain the whole time she'd lived with her mother. Now, with her husband by her side, she tore the package open and **saw the face of her father** for the first time since she was one month old.

Ada seemed quite calm. She didn't rush off to write any poems; in fact, she didn't react the way Annabella had dreaded at all.

She shrugged, and looked around for somewhere to hang the picture. A satisfied Dr. King reported to Annabella that Ada was OK.

He might have spoken too soon.

Four Shillings Down

In October 1835, the newlyweds spent a few days apart for the first time in their three-month-long marriage. Ada took a break with Annabella in Southampton—at the horse races.

When she was very little, Ada had been afraid of horses. But she'd overcome her fear and discovered that riding actually helped her with the nervous attacks she'd had ever since that early bout of measles, in 1829. Now she loved to gallop around the estate. So, a day in horsey company seemed like a great idea.

Horse racing was heavily tied up with gambling, of course, and **gambling horrified Annabella**. It reminded her of Byron squandering money they didn't have. But while ladies were never supposed to gamble with cards or visit a casino, betting on horses was considered acceptable. So off they went.

Somehow, Ada became separated from Annabella in the crowd. She spotted a bookie (a man taking bets) standing next to a board, with a list of names of horses, and numbers written next to them. Horses *and* numbers? Ada was intrigued.

She had four shillings in her purse. Her heart beat a little more quickly. Somewhere, very deep inside of her, Byron might have been calling, urging her to give it a try.

Ada bet the four shillings. She guessed which horses would win. She guessed *wrong*. She lost.

Later, she told William everything, but she assured him that no way was she going to get into gambling. And, at the time, she really believed it.

KIDS AND CHOLERA

In May 1836, Ada and William's first child was born. Annabella was so happy to have a grandson that she even suggested a name for him that Ada wasn't expecting at all . . .

In September 1837, young Byron was followed by . . .

. . . and finally in July 1839, Ralph.

Shortly after little Annabella was born, Ada caught cholera, a very dangerous disease that's caused by . . . well, there's no nice way to say this. It's caused by drinking water that's contaminated with . . . poop! In those days, before modern toilets and sewers, cholera was very common and could **kill its victims within a day**. First they'd feel sick and dizzy, but within a few hours . . . well, let's just say that fluid came spurting out of every hole in the body that fluid can spurt out of, and they'd die of dehydration. Ew!

Ada was one of the lucky ones. She recovered, but the illness really wore her out.

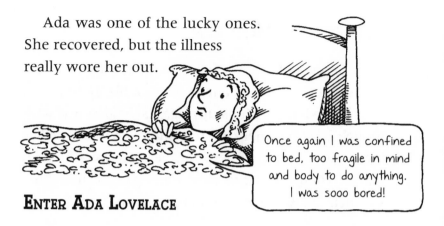

Once again I was confined to bed, too fragile in mind and body to do anything. I was sooo bored!

ENTER ADA LOVELACE

At this time, Ada got the name we know her by today. In June 1838, the young Queen Victoria was crowned and a whole lot of new lordly titles were created to celebrate.

The title of Lord Lovelace had died out with Ada's distant relatives, the Noel family. Under Victoria, the title made a comeback, and William and Ada found themselves renamed and retitled.

Just call me Ada Lovelace.

Lord William King-Noel, 1st Earl of Lovelace

Lady Augusta Ada King-Noel, Countess of Lovelace

Mesmerized by Mesmerism

For four uncomfortable years, Ada was mostly either expecting a baby, looking after a baby, or ill. There wasn't much time left over for studying. Maybe that was why, though she loved her children, **she found it hard to like them**. They distracted her from her first love—mathematics. Then she found something that fascinated her so much she was able to combine her illness with study.

German scientist Franz Mesmer believed there was an invisible force that could improve human health. He called this force animal magnetism, or mesmerism (a bit like hypnotism today, with a bit of psychology thrown in), and his experimental cures began **causing quite a stir** in Europe. In the 1830s, mesmerism began to take off in England, stirring up a "mesmerism mania." Ada was fascinated too; she watched demonstrations and tried some experiments, including a famous one called the Oscillating Shilling, which demonstrated invisible forces.

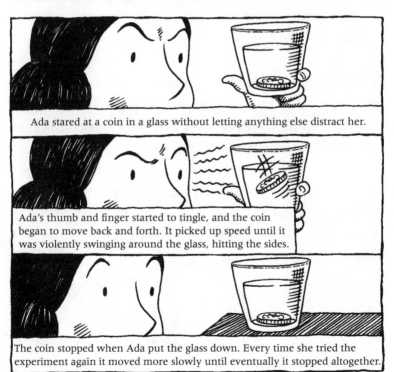

Ada stared at a coin in a glass without letting anything else distract her.

Ada's thumb and finger started to tingle, and the coin began to move back and forth. It picked up speed until it was violently swinging around the glass, hitting the sides.

The coin stopped when Ada put the glass down. Every time she tried the experiment again it moved more slowly until eventually it stopped altogether.

Ultimately, Ada found that mesmerism did give her some pain relief, but didn't really help her recover. She got better the more traditional way: with lots of rest. She didn't completely rule mesmerism out, though.

BACK TO WORK

Ada finally felt well enough to return to math in 1840. She was twenty-four and Ralph was four months old. She had kept up her friendship with Babbage all this time—and started to have ideas of her own.

She and Babbage had both thought of the Difference Engine as no more than a very clever calculating machine that helped engineers do complicated equations. Babbage still thought this, but Ada was starting to see—very faintly—how math could help us with the kind of things our computers do today. Ada's imagination, which Annabella had tried so hard to erase, was making larger and larger leaps, turning Ada into **a true visionary**. She had no idea how ahead of her time she was. Sadly, neither did anyone else.

So science can be used to design things! Very interesting.

A TREATISE ON MECHANICS, APPLIED TO THE ARTS
Including Statics and Hydrostatics

Solitaire has thousands of possible outcomes.

Meanwhile, science was still churning out new device after new device. The latest wonder-invention was the electric telegraph—the closest the nineteenth century came to texting, or online shopping. An electric pulse sent a coded message along a wire, which could be received at the other end of the wire.

A letter from London would take **at least a day** to reach Ada, whereas a telegram arrived the same day (though it did have to be delivered by hand from the telegraph office). That would make it easy for Ada to place an order or let William know she'd missed her train.

Ada realized that bringing to life all the amazing gadgets that were making the world an easier place to live required a combination of scientific knowledge and a creative mind. She called this combination "poetical science."

The world was so exciting that Ada actually worried that it might all get too much for her. By now, she was pretty certain she *had* an imagination, despite Annabella's efforts, though perhaps it was becoming a little too active. A feeling had been growing inside Ada for some time, and it was this:

My desire to be a mathematician came from above.

By exploring math and science Ada felt she could help other people to understand God's creations, and even understand God himself. She just had to find a way to carry out her mission . . .

Which is where Babbage came in. While Ada had been having babies, he'd been working on a huge steel baby of his own. It would be **bigger and better** than the Difference Engine, and her work on it with him would eventually make Ada famous.

5   ANALYTICAL ADA

Babbage was worried that his beloved Difference Engine just wasn't good enough. It was slow. You had to know some of the answers in advance to make it work out the rest—and if the human got those first answers wrong, so did the machine. You had to reset it at the end of every calculation. It didn't have a memory, so you couldn't reuse a number without entering it by hand. And worst of all . . .

It can be **inaccurate!**

Even if the human operator got their calculations exactly right, there were some numbers the Difference Engine just couldn't handle. For instance, what is 1 divided by 3? The answer is $1/3$, but the Difference Engine couldn't say that. It would have to say 0.3, but that answer is only *almost* right. Multiply it back again, and the answer you get is 0.9, not 1. The *real* answer is 0.3333333 etc.—which is a recurring decimal, and the Difference Engine couldn't handle recurring decimals. It ran out of wheels. But those teeny-tiny differences in the numbers could lead to **absolutely humungous** ones later on.

Difference Engine No. 2 was meant to be bigger and better than Difference Engine No. 1, but it had exactly the same problems. Babbage wasn't about to give up, though, oh no! He started devising **a whole new machine** instead.

PLANS FOR THE ANALYTICAL ENGINE

Designed by: C. Babbage Esq.
Weight: 4 tons, about the same as a small railway engine.
Dimensions: 15 feet high (4.5 meters). Length depends on number of columns in the Store, but at least 10 feet (3 meters).
Moving parts: 20,000 wheels and many more levers, gears and switches.
Power source: steam, of course—it was too heavy to crank by hand.

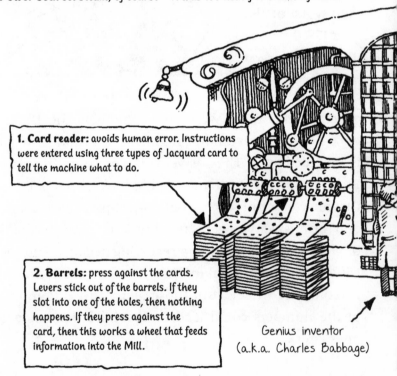

1. Card reader: avoids human error. Instructions were entered using three types of Jacquard card to tell the machine what to do.

2. Barrels: press against the cards. Levers stick out of the barrels. If they slot into one of the holes, then nothing happens. If they press against the card, then this works a wheel that feeds information into the Mill.

Genius inventor
(a.k.a. Charles Babbage)

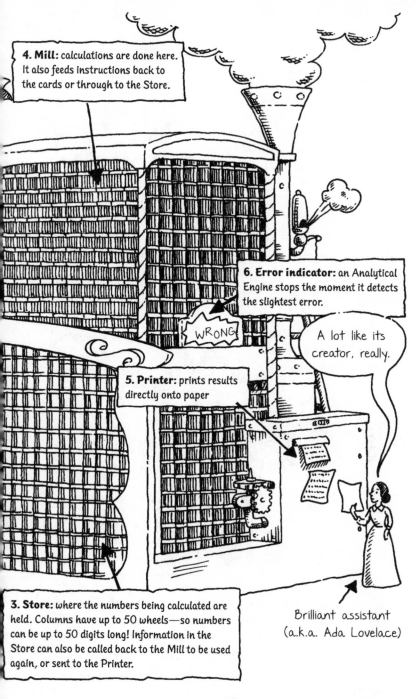

4. **Mill:** calculations are done here. It also feeds instructions back to the cards or through to the Store.

6. **Error indicator:** an Analytical Engine stops the moment it detects the slightest error.

A lot like its creator, really.

WRONG

5. **Printer:** prints results directly onto paper

3. **Store:** where the numbers being calculated are held. Columns have up to 50 wheels—so numbers can be up to 50 digits long! Information in the Store can also be called back to the Mill to be used again, or sent to the Printer.

Brilliant assistant (a.k.a. Ada Lovelace)

SOUND FAMILIAR?

The Analytical Engine had a memory. It could process numbers. It could even work on its own! Sound familiar?

Babbage only called his machine the Analytical Engine because the word *computer* meant something slightly different. In those days a computer wasn't a thing, it was a human being paid to do very complicated calculations, or computations . . .

Teams of (usually) men were employed to do different kinds of calculations.

Working out orbits of the Moon.

Working out how much the Earth wobbles as it spins.

Producing a table of high and low tides around the world for next year.

Put the answers to lots of small calculations together and you can answer much larger calculations—probably the only time a roomful of men will come up with something useful.

The Analytical Engine could do those large sums all on its own. It had hardware (the Mill, the Store, the Barrels) and software (the cards). It might have been mechanical and steam-powered, but the Analytical Engine was actually a clockwork computer: **the first computer ever designed**, and over 100 years ahead of its time!

It was amazing, and it wasn't just good for number-crunching—Ada saw so many other ways it could be used. The Analytical Engine could make Britain a world leader in science, in art, in engineering—in any field you can think of. There was just one small problem. Like the Difference Engine No. 2, the Analytical Engine **didn't actually exist** . . . yet.

Building it would take money. (Babbage was a very rich man, but he wasn't *that* rich.) The British government had already given him a lot of money, and all Babbage had produced was a demonstration model. So they wouldn't be coughing up any more cash without a very good reason.

Babbage needed to find another way to pay for his Analytical Engine. People needed to know about it and understand what it could do, the difference it could make. **It needed publicity**.

Babbage definitely wasn't the person to do this. He had horrible people skills and *really* couldn't handle stupid questions.

Whoever tried to publicize the Analytical Engine would have to answer a lot of questions, many of them stupid.

Babbage needed someone who understood:

a) him;

b) the Analytical Engine; and

c) other people.

It was the perfect job for Ada. She just had to decide how she was going to do it.

6   ADA MAKES SOME NOTES

In fall 1840, just as Ada was taking up math again, Babbage was invited to Turin, Italy, to talk to some Italian scientists about the Analytical Engine. The Italians loved him and he loved them. They treated Babbage as a great mathematician, scientist, and engineer, which was exactly how he thought he should be treated back in England (and wasn't).

One of the scientists, Luigi Federico Menabrea, was so impressed by Babbage's talk that he wrote and published an article about it in October 1842.

The article was pretty much word for word what Babbage had said in his Turin speech, so he got the details right, but Ada found it . . . disappointing. Menabrea had copied Babbage so carefully that the article **hardly made any sense** to a non-genius, i.e., most anyone. Besides, it had been published in a European journal, in French. This wouldn't help Ada publicize the Analytical Engine, but it did give her an idea.

I speak French. I'll translate the article and publish it in English!

But it still won't make sense to most people.

Then I'll just add a couple of notes at the end.

ADA BECOMES NOTE-ORIOUS

Babbage couldn't understand why Ada didn't just write her own article. Ada didn't do that because . . . um . . . well, to be honest, it just didn't occur to her. In the end, Ada's Notes (and they deserve a capital N) were two and a half times longer than the article!

She wrote seven Notes in total. By now, most scientists and mathematicians had heard of the Difference Engine, so first they needed to know what made the Difference Engine and the Analytical Engine, er . . . different.

This is, roughly, how Ada explained it in Note A:

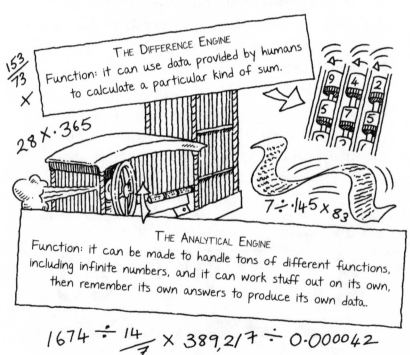

Even Babbage was impressed when he read Note A.

It demonstrates a depth of understanding that even I did not anticipate.

Babbage still thought of the Analytical Engine as just a massive, and massively impressive, calculating machine that would help Victorian bridge-building engineers, ship designers, and steam-engine manufacturers get their figures exactly right.

But Ada approached it with **poetical science**. By combining her scientific knowledge and understanding with her imagination, she saw things differently:

Well, in Ada's mind, music was just a series of different sounds, put together mathematically.

Notes progress in a pattern, which is another way of saying they're a mathematical sequence.

Pictures could be broken down into **mathematically described shapes and colors**. If something was mathematical—and almost everything is—then the Analytical Engine could handle it.

Pictures can be divided into areas that are proportionate to each other in size.

The Analytical Engine weaves algebraic patterns just as the Jacquard loom weaves flowers and leaves.

Even Babbage, who had had the idea for this amazing machine, didn't get Ada's way of thinking. He may have invented the computer, but **it was Ada who realized what computers could do**. In the middle of the nineteenth century, Ada Lovelace had just invented the idea of digital music and computer graphics. OK, so there was no computer advanced enough to play them on, but even so—WOW!

THINK OF A NUMBER SEQUENCE

In Note B, Ada described how the Analytical Engine's hardware, the Store and Mill, worked—and right away she introduced her readers to a whole new concept. Until now, all the cogs and wheels of mechanical machines—from a basic clock to the Difference Engine, and anything in between—were designed to do just one job. But in the Analytical Engine, all those cogs and wheels could be made to do *different* things, often at the same time. That was amazing enough on its own, but what was even more amazing was that they **didn't need a human** to tell them what to do. The machine could do its own thinking.

Ada just needed a killer demonstration to show what the Analytical Engine was capable of. She thought of the most difficult calculation she could set . . . the most complicated mathematical pattern it could weave.

Bernoulli numbers are so ridiculously, ludicrously complex that Ada didn't fully understand them and even the Difference Engine couldn't manage them. She had to ask Babbage for the *extremely* complicated equation that is normally used.

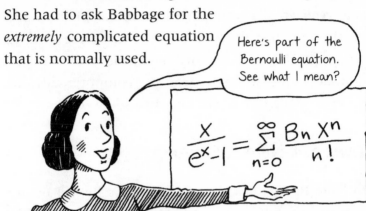

So now, for Note G, she had the **incredibly challenging** task of making the Analytical Engine calculate Bernoulli numbers. First, she had to make the equation understandable to the Analytical Engine, and then she had to make it understandable to the average reader, so they would get what she was doing.

Today, mathematicians use Bernoulli numbers to calculate how air flows over and under airplane wings in flight.

Ada's Input

Writing the Notes meant that, for the first time, Ada gave Babbage's plans for the Analytical Engine a long, hard look with her analytical mind. Whenever she spotted an error, Ada fed it back to Babbage so that Babbage could improve the design. At one point, she noticed an error in the mechanism for working out equations; at another, she realized Babbage was wrong about the number of cards needed. Together, Ada and Babbage polished up the idea of the Analytical Engine and **made it even better**.

Ada was enjoying herself! But if she'd had her way, her contribution would have been the Analytical Engine's best-kept secret.

Ada didn't want her name on the article because

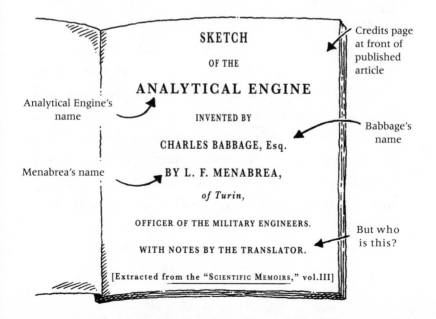

Credits page at front of published article

Analytical Engine's name

Babbage's name

Menabrea's name

But who is this?

SKETCH

OF THE

ANALYTICAL ENGINE

INVENTED BY

CHARLES BABBAGE, Esq.

BY L. F. MENABREA,

of Turin,

OFFICER OF THE MILITARY ENGINEERS.

WITH NOTES BY THE TRANSLATOR.

[Extracted from the "SCIENTIFIC MEMOIRS," vol.III]

she still saw herself as **Babbage's humble servant**. As with her dad's bestselling poem, she didn't want to get rich on the back of the article, because lords and ladies were not supposed to earn money. Additionally, the Lovelace family motto was *Labor ipse voluptas*—"Labor is its own reward."

But even though he was a lord, William thought Ada should take the credit. She was the one who had made the translation, after all. The Notes could be the first step in her mathematical career, he pointed out—but only if Ada admitted she'd written them. It was just publicity; no money would be changing hands so it didn't count as paid work.

In the end, Ada reluctantly signed each page of the Notes with her initials, A. A. L.

Note G

Ada worked on the translation and the Notes for nearly a year, but Note G is the one she's most remembered for, because it's where she broke the Bernoulli equation down into lots of simpler equations. She put each one into a row of a table. Running a number through each of the simpler equations in turn would give the same result as using the full equation from the start. Ada's system worked just like a team of human computers.

Her table looked something like this:

Ada just called her table a table. But to modern eyes, it's a list of machine-readable instructions. Ada had gone and written **the world's first ever computer program**! Which made Ada Lovelace, an aristocratic lady living in Victorian England, the world's first computer programmer!

THE BABBAGE FACTOR

Babbage was 100 percent behind Ada, and gave her a lot of helpful advice. But working with him still wasn't easy. In fact, thanks to him, the Notes very nearly didn't get published. Babbage was so absent-minded that he managed to lose some of the pages when Ada sent them to him for approval. Ada was so angry she nearly forgot she was a lady!

This was long before photocopiers had been invented, so Ada had to **rewrite the whole thing from memory**.

Then Babbage decided he wanted to write a preface (or introduction) to the article, to tell everyone what it was about. Ada thought that would be fine, since the machine was his baby. She must have forgotten what Babbage was like . . . until she read what he had written. All those little irritations that had built up over the years, especially his treatment by the British government, had come pouring out.

To top it all off, he asked Ada to sign what he'd written, so **it would look like she had written it** herself! Ada refused point-blank. She said it would be suicidal. Babbage threatened to pull the whole article . . . It was nearly the end of their friendship.

But ultimately, it was Ada's article, not Babbage's. So she left his preface out. The article and the Notes were published in September 1843, in a journal called *Scientific Memoirs*. Babbage's ranty piece was published in another magazine.

And that was it. A whole year of hard work all done. Even Babbage was impressed enough to stop sulking and gush with praise.

She is the Enchantress of Number. She has thrown her magical spell around mathematics and has grasped it with a force that few masculine intellects could have exerted.

In other words, he thought she was brilliant with numbers and even better than most men! So now Ada could sit back and enjoy fame and fortune, while the Analytical Engine finally got built, ushering in the Computer Age in the middle of the nineteenth century. Right? *Wrong*.

7   AGENT ADA

Unfortunately, on the November 11, 1842, eleven months before the Notes were published, Babbage had met with the prime minister of Great Britain to try to persuade him to fund his new machine. **The meeting had not gone well**.

Convincing Sir Robert was never going to be easy. He was a busy man, and he had already made up his mind on the Analytical Engine very clear indeed. But there was still a chance the meeting could have worked.

Here's how Ada would have handled it:

We've had some terrible harvests, so food prices are high. There could be a famine!

Fear not, Prime Minister, the Analytical Engine can help you organize agriculture and plan food distribution.

I want to limit child labor without losing out on profits from our industries. Factory workers ages nine to thirteen should work shorter hours and get a break for lunch.

The Analytical Engine could help you plan a program that's fair to workers while keeping factories prosperous.

I have an empire to run! An army! A navy!

The Analytical Engine can help work out how to get our soldiers and ships wherever they're needed! And the money you'll save will pay for the cost of the machine!

Marvellous!

Then you shall have all the funding you need, Lady Lovelace!

Here's roughly what actually happened when Babbage met the prime minister:

That was that. There was no chance of getting any money out of the government now. When Ada found out, she couldn't believe her ears. Babbage was in trouble—but she *could* see a way out.

ADA'S OFFER

Ada really believed that Babbage's machine could change the world, but she knew it was going to take more than his brilliant engineering skills to make it happen. So, she decided to **make him an offer he couldn't refuse**. On Monday August 14, 1843, she sat down to write the most important letter of her life.

By now, she knew how Babbage's mind worked, so she made the letter all about *him*. She talked about how brilliant he was, how busy he must be, and she suggested that he should dedicate his colossal intellect to the creation of the Analytical Engine, while she handled *everything* else. The final part of her (sixteen-page) letter boiled down to these three questions:

1. Will you let me deal with other people at all times?

> After that interview with the prime minister, the fewer people Babbage met, the better.

2. Will you deal with technical problems I identify as soon as I identify them?

> There were some technical problems only Babbage could handle, but he had a habit of ignoring everyone else's concerns. I needed him to answer any questions I raised.

3. If I come up with a publicity plan for the Analytical Engine, will you back it all the way?

> I knew I could skillfully direct his time and energy; I just needed him to follow that direction. Easier said than done with Babbage!

Ada would flatter and charm people, instead of becoming hostile. She had social skills enough for the two of them. No one ever left a meeting with Ada feeling angry and upset (apart from Babbage). She'd find backers prepared to give them the money to build the Analytical Engine. She would make sure cash was always available when it was needed. She would direct his engineers, and make sure they were happy in their work.

In short, **Ada was offering to become Babbage's agent**, a project manager for every part of his life, helping to make the Analytical Engine become real. And what's more—because *Labor ipse voluptas*—he wouldn't have to pay her a penny.

Ada made the offer with great visions for the future, secretly hoping she'd eventually be able to start pointing the Analytical Engine at non-mathematical problems, like art and music—maybe even poetry.

The Computer Age was just around the corner. Ada could feel it coming. This had to be the mission that God had given her and she was absolutely ready to throw herself at it. She just needed Babbage to say yes.

Babbage didn't write back. He went to see Ada in person the very next day. She was so nervous. She expected some discussion, maybe some fine-tuning of her conditions into something Babbage felt he could work with.

Babbage's diary for the next day states his answer very bluntly.

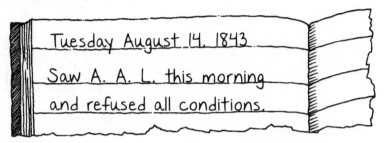

Tuesday August 14, 1843
Saw A. A. L. this morning and refused all conditions.

But why? We know Babbage totally trusted Ada's mathematical abilities, or he wouldn't have called her the "Enchantress of Number." We know he thought her Notes were brilliant, but maybe that was the problem. From now on, if people didn't understand what he was talking about, Babbage could just point them in the direction of the Notes, and bingo! He wouldn't need Ada to convince them to pay for his machine once they understood his genius.

And all the other possibilities Ada saw for the Analytical Engine—the art, the music, etc.—well, Babbage just didn't get them.

Ada was **incredibly disappointed** by his answer, but she didn't give up hope right away. After all, no one had actually read her Notes yet—the article hadn't been published. Maybe that would help. She'd just have to wait for publication day.

Slowly, September 1843 came around . . .

BUT SHE'S JUST A WOMAN!

The Notes were a work of genius. They showed that the author had a brilliant mathematical mind. But people didn't **realize** who the author was right away. When they did, some quickly changed their tune:

Thankfully, Babbage himself told people outright that Ada hadn't just written the Notes—she'd actually corrected some of his mistakes too!

And I wouldn't say that if I didn't mean it!

Luckily, many of the people who mattered—the scientists and mathematicians—read the Notes, and nodded in agreement.

In the end, though, it didn't matter how great Ada said the Analytical Engine *could* be. If the machine didn't exist, it wouldn't do any of the brilliant things she'd explained. Now that Babbage had ruined things with the Prime Minister and refused Ada's offer—well, it looked highly unlikely that the machine would ever exist.

ADA DEPRESSED

With all Ada's hope and optimism crushed, her illness made a sudden comeback. Her weight went up and down, and her physical and mental health just kept on going *down*.

From the outside, apart from the disappointment of the Analytical Engine, **Ada's life looked practically perfect.** She was still young—not even thirty yet. She had three fine children and a husband who loved her.

She had her music and her horse riding. She had her pets—a pair of dogs, Sprite and Nelson, and a collection of birds—that she loved so much she let them roam freely around the house.

She moved in high society, with rich and amazing friends: writers like William Wordsworth and Charles Dickens, famous people like the Duke of Wellington, and scientists like Michael Faraday.

But Ada desperately wanted to be part of the new age of scientific discovery, and it seemed she was being left behind. **She grew so depressed** that her mind felt as paralyzed as her body had been when she was a child. Why couldn't she *do* anything?

Soon, her home life wasn't going too well either. After ten years of marriage, William still let her pursue her studies, still gave her an allowance, and still really loved her. Ada desperately wanted to love him back, but **the spark just wasn't there**, and there was nothing William could do about it. It wasn't his fault, though, Ada had never really wanted a husband in the first place. The children hadn't improved things either. When they were little, Ada had loved them without liking them. Now that she was ill again, she even had difficulty loving them.

Unfortunately, every year adds to my utter want of pleasure in my children. They are to me irksome duties, and nothing more.

A modern doctor would probably say that Ada was suffering from depression, which can affect the body as well as the mind. When her regular doctor visited at the end of 1844, he said she had "a mad look" so horrible that he would never forget it and he immediately prescribed her twenty-five drops of laudanum, a foul-tasting mixture of opium and wine that reduced pain, but also took away the patient's ability to think clearly.

Today's doctors would never dream of prescribing such a harmful and addictive drug for depression, but on this occasion, strangely, the laudanum seemed to work. After a year of nothing happening, Ada felt able to take control of her thoughts again.

When Life Gives You Lemons . . .

In fact, Ada started to wonder whether her illness was the answer. Soon after her recovery, **she had her next great idea**.

If scientists could map the planets and their movements, maybe they could map the human mind too?

Well, she could be the first to try . . .

CALCULUS OF THE NERVOUS SYSTEM

Or, a mathematical map of the human mind
Outline of ideas by Ada Lovelace

Question: How do thoughts and feelings arise in the brain?

Answer: We don't know.

We believe that:

All things are made of atoms.

Atoms are held together by by electric and magnetic forces.

Therefore so is the brain.

Can the two somehow work together??

Aim: To create a mathematical model of how the brain works
Materials: The laboratory of my mind—i.e., my own brain

I shall work out a law or laws for the mutual actions of the molecules of the brain.

It was a great idea and it shows just how unstoppable Ada was when she put her mind to it, but, over 150 years later, even with modern medical imaging, scientists **still aren't "brainy" enough to work it out.**

MYSTICAL, MESMERIZING MAGNETISM

While Ada's thoughts were in this direction, she wondered if mesmerism was worth another look. The practice was all about invisible forces, and whatever it was that made the brain work had to be an invisible force too. She hadn't given mesmerism much thought since she'd recovered from cholera, but it definitely interested her now.

If mesmerism was real, Ada reckoned it probably had something to do with electricity. Victorian scientists knew that electric currents run along the body's nerves and make muscles work because of an experiment by Italian scientist Luigi Galvani.

Ada wanted to properly test mesmerism, and she thought she knew how. She decided to write an article on the German scientist Karl von Reichenbach, who claimed that some mesmerized patients produced "luminous emanations" when they were exposed to magnetism—in other words, **they glowed**!

So many of the claims about mesmerism were impossible to prove, but Ada thought this one could be tested. If a patient *said* she was feeling better, she may not be telling the truth, but, *if* mesmerism made her glow, anyone could see it.

> Science says that if something is scientifically true then it is **always** true, no exceptions, it doesn't matter who says otherwise, and you can prove it by experimenting. You can say, in advance, "If I do THIS, then THAT will happen," and it does.

Ada wanted to test Reichenbach's claim using a new sort of science that was just taking off: **the science of photography**.

> Stop talking and hold that pose for another five minutes . . .

> People were actually managing to capture images and store them on bits of glass or paper or metal treated with certain chemicals—it was incredible!

A photograph should show whether people glowed during mesmerism and then the amount of light could be measured and graded. Mesmerism could be put to the test once and for all.

It was a great idea, but sadly Ada's article was never published, and, as far as we know, no one ever tried her experiment. Something positive did come from it, though. Ada suddenly felt a whole lot better. Focusing on a serious piece of science—the thing she enjoyed more than anything else—had improved her health dramatically. Her depression lifted and, wonderfully, she found she could actually enjoy being a mom again!

So it's kind of a shame that after years and years of having very good ideas, her new energy and purpose now brought mostly **seriously awful ones**.

8 ADA AND THE HORSES

By 1845, it was pretty clear that **Ada's future did not include the Analytical Engine**. Without funding, and without Ada's project management, Babbage's work on it had totally stalled.

Science was still Ada's religion. She still felt she was on a mission from God, but she was having difficulty figuring out what He wanted her to do next. So she tried a few things out . . .

Before marrying William, Ada had experimented with a design for a women's swimsuit. Women didn't really go swimming in those days—they just waded out into the water, paddled about a bit, and waded back—and there was a good reason for that . . .

Usual swimsuit:
- Petticoats fill up with air. If the lower half starts to float, the woman falls over.
- Impossible to swim in.

One-piece suit designed by Ada:
- No inflating petticoats.
- Swimming is possible.

It was a practical idea, but Ada's future definitely did not lie in fashion design.

Perhaps William could help. He'd written an article about growing crops, and Ada added some technical footnotes about using a nebulometer, which was a machine for measuring daylight.

Still sunny.

But working with William was nowhere near as exciting as working out a program for a clockwork computer. She had a brilliant mind, and she wanted to use it. For Ada, it was numbers or nothing!

She'd been friends with Babbage for over ten years now and even though things hadn't worked out with the Analytical Engine, the two of them still loved to talk about math and bounce ideas off each other. Years earlier, Ada had discussed the math of Solitaire, a game for one player that involves moving pegs on a board until only one is left. Ada thought she could create a language that would apply math to games so she could **win any game by working it out mathematically**.

She was thinking **way ahead of everyone else**, again, having ideas that that wouldn't be realized for another century. Little did she know that one day a computer language would be named after her, which would do far more important stuff than playing games.

While Ada was thinking about Solitaire, Babbage had vague plans for something like an automatic tic-tac-toe machine. It would have been the first ever gadget where you could enter a move and the machine would play against you. It could have been the ancestor to today's handheld games!

Step right up.
A penny a game!

There are 26,830 possible games
that can be played on this grid.

No thanks, it's easier with
chalk and pavement.

Babbage thought he might raise money for the Analytical Engine by displaying the games machine at fairs, and offering members of the public the chance to play on it. Ada encouraged him, hoping his machine would *produce the silver and golden somethings*—enough money, in other words—to develop the Analytical Engine further.

Sadly, their gaming ideas didn't pan out. Babbage's butterfly mind fluttered off in yet another new direction, and Ada had other things to worry about. She hadn't been joking about those silver and golden somethings. Money was starting to press on her mind . . .

MONEY, MONEY, MONEY

Despite ten years of marriage, William still gave Ada the same allowance of £300 each year (about $20,000 today). It was worth a lot less by then than it had been at the start. By contrast Annabella had a far more impressive income of £7,000 a year (about $500,000 today).

Remember the four-shilling bet she'd lost way back at the horse track? **Ada hadn't forgotten the excitement of it.** Now, without the distraction of a project, the bit of Byron in her she'd tried so hard to suppress was creeping back. She started spending some of her allowance to bet on the horses.

Gambling is all down to probability, and probability is part of math. I'm very good at math, so what can possibly go wrong?

Quite a lot, actually.

How Horse Racing Works (Very Briefly)

SEACOOKIE 5-1

Five pounds on Seacookie, please.

FIDDLE
SPEED
CHAM
LIGHT
GLUE F

Bookies work out how likely Seacookie is to win. The odds on Seacookie are 5–1.

If Ada bets $5 on Seacookie to win and the horse does win, she gets $25 (five times what she bet). And she gets back the $5 she paid.

But if Seacookie loses, she loses her $5.

But I know I can win next time. Just one more try . . .

And *that* was where Ada went wrong.

If Ada had inherited her father's impulse to gamble, she'd also inherited his poor choice of winners. **She kept on losing**. She lost so much that she had to borrow money from the banks to pay her debts. By 1850, she owed the banks £500 (about $35,000 today), which was £200 more than her annual income. So she borrowed a few hundred from Annabella to pay the bank back.

I . . . er . . . need it for my . . . er . . . traveling fund.

TAKING A BREAK

In 1848, maybe because of the stress of the gambling losses, **Ada's aches and pains were back**, and her heart was beating in strange, irregular ways. Today we'd say she was having palpitations. She tried various remedies, but the symptoms didn't go away.

Finally, in 1850, deciding that a break would be good for her health, William and Ada took a vacation, touring the north of England.

Among other places, they visited Newstead Abbey, in Nottinghamshire. Byron had lived there, and it was where he was buried. So, Newstead was Ada's family home, though, of course, **Annabella had never taken her there**. This was Ada's first visit, and she absolutely loved it.

Newstead was now owned by Thomas Wildman, an old school friend of Byron's, and he was more than happy to show the Lovelaces around. **He even talked to Ada about her father**, and she discovered a few things that the two of them had in common:

🖋 They both enjoyed swimming. That's why Ada had designed her swimsuit. In 1810, Byron had become the first man to swim from Europe to Asia, across the Hellespont in Turkey—two and a half miles —through very treacherous water.

🖋 They both sometimes had difficulty controlling their weight.

🖋 They both loved animals. Ada was delighted to discover that, just like her, Byron had let animals wander around his home. Except, while Ada had a couple of dogs, a parrot, and some starlings, his menagerie had included eight dogs, some tortoises, a hedgehog, three monkeys, five cats, an eagle, a crow, a falcon—oh, and a bear.

When Byron discovered he couldn't bring his wolfhound to college, he had turned up with a bear instead.

·PORTER·

It doesn't say anything about bears here.

YIKES!

And, as it turned out, Ada and Byron both loved Newstead.

Something in the landscape, the woods, and the great halls of the ancient building itself, seemed to speak to Ada. It was as if **her father's side of her soul was waking up**.

For years Ada had been afraid of her dad. Now, suddenly, she didn't feel scared anymore. She'd discovered he wasn't all bad. Even Annabella had to agree that he had been on the side of the poor and oppressed: the reason he'd been in Greece when he died was because he was helping the Greeks fight for their independence. Ada began to realize that she really wasn't worried about turning out like him.

The Lovelace Losers

William left Newstead to go and attend to some boring agricultural business, and Ada was left alone. She took herself to the Doncaster Racecourse, and finally threw all caution to the wind. Her favorite horse, Voltigeur, was running, and she bet on him to win—not for any clever mathematical reasons, but because he belonged to a friend. It was just the kind of thing her father would have done. And, believe it or not, **Voltigeur won!**

Next, Ada went to the Epsom Derby, one of the most important horse races of the year. The good news: she bet on Voltigeur again, and he won again. The bad news: she also backed several losers. By the end of the day **she'd lost a lot more than she'd won**.

She knew she had to tell William that she was in debt. But unfortunately, William couldn't do much to help without going to Annabella.

FEELING THE PINCH

Even though her daughter had been married for ten years, Annabella couldn't quite let go. She cunningly kept a bit of control the only way she could: by managing the couple's money.

William owned properties that were worth a lot, but getting ahold of large amounts of cash was harder than you'd think. He'd been promised plenty of money when he married Ada, but Annabella only **paid out small amounts**, bit by bit. It was enough for William and Ada to live on, but for anything extra they had to ask Annabella. Because Annabella held the family purse strings, she could tighten— or loosen—them as she pleased.

Please, Mother, can we have some money?

Hmm, let me see . . .

When one of the Lovelace houses needed repairs, for example, Annabella told William to pay for the work and promised to pay him back. He hired the workmen to do their thing, but Annabella really took her time handing over the money.

Now Annabella was smelling a rat. She soon worked out that her daughter was in debt, so when Ada produced a long list of expenses, Annabella took a long, hard look.

Eventually Annabella agreed to pay for some items, but it wasn't enough to pay off the rest of Ada's gambling debts. In desperation, Ada hit on an idea that would get them all their money back, big time. **It involved a bit more gambling**, but the money she'd win would be huge.

No married woman had much cash in those days, so to convince the bookies she could afford the bets, Ada needed William on her side. He just had to sign a little letter . . .

William agreed, but he was making a big mistake.

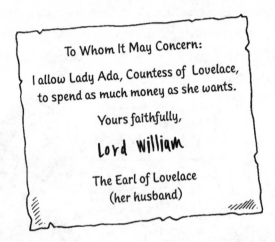

To Whom It May Concern:

I allow Lady Ada, Countess of Lovelace, to spend as much money as she wants.

Yours faithfully,

Lord William

The Earl of Lovelace
(her husband)

FOOLISHLY FOOLPROOF

Ada reckoned she'd worked out a foolproof system for winning bets. She convinced a group of five friends to join with her in a gambling syndicate. They would share what they won between them. That way, **they could spend more money on bigger bets**, and get even bigger winnings back. At least, that was the idea.

Ada was the syndicate's bookie, so she set the odds and paid out the winnings. When it came to losses, she had to pay for those herself.

The sensible thing would have been to spread the syndicate's bets over several different horses—some would lose, but others might win—then overall they wouldn't lose much money. But Ada didn't do that. Oh no. At the York Spring Meeting of 1851, she put nearly *all* the syndicate's money on her favorite horse, Voltigeur . . . and Voltigeur lost.

So, Ada's foolproof system turned out to be extremely foolish. In desperation, she tried to win all the money back at the Derby on May 21. She had just enough money left to make it work—if she won. This time she bet on several horses, just in case.

They *all* lost. Ada now owed over **ten times her annual income**. To pay that back from her allowance, she'd have to spend nothing for the next ten years and eight months!

At first, she didn't dare tell William. But soon she had to. Most of that money was owed to a man named Malcolm. Malcolm was even more broke than Ada was and he started making threats:

Ada was horrified. Everyone knew her father had been forced out of the country because of his debts. That didn't happen anymore, but still, a gentleman— or in this case, a lady—was expected to behave honorably. Ada knew she'd have to pay up, if she wanted to keep her reputation. **She had no choice but to tell William _everything_**.

After that, things became a little bit tense in the Lovelace household, to say the least. William thought through his options and agreed to pay Malcolm off. He didn't want to disgrace his wife, however foolish she'd been.

He didn't pay up right away, but he did pay eventually, so at least Ada could breathe again. And being honest about the debts brought her and William closer together. There were still tough times ahead, but she felt sure they could get through them as a couple.

Let's put it all behind us.

In fact, in the same month as her disastrous Derby losses, something happened that made her feel very positive about the future.

9   ADA'S FINAL ADVENTURE

In May 1851, Ada and William were off to the opening of the Great Exhibition in London, followed by a ball at Buckingham Palace that was hosted by Queen Victoria and Prince Albert, no less.

Exhibition featured the world's first ever pay-to-use public toilets. The cost was a penny.

Venue: the Crystal Palace, a 1800-foot-long glass pavilion in Hyde Park

TOILETS
A PENNY A GO

Hurry up!

Average daily attendance: 43,000 people, from farmworkers to lords and ladies

THE GREAT EXHIBITION

- Held May 1 to October 15, 1851 to highlight the excellence of invention and manufacturing in Britain and around the world.

- Total attendance: Six million people (one third of the population of Britain).

- Number of exhibits: 100,000 with ten miles of display space.

- Exhibits included: scientific instruments, musical instruments, works of art, and weaponry.

All the latest scientific inventions were there. The Analytical Engine should have been exhibited too, except, of course, it didn't exist. Even so, surrounded by the greatest science of the greatest country on Earth, **Ada was thrilled.**

The Crystal Palace itself was poetical science in action. It looked beautiful. Ada would have made the trip just to see it. She had read about most of the exhibits, but this was the first time she got to see the science she had learned about actually being put into use. Clever people had used their imaginations to come up with some brand-new things—it was all so exciting.

The Great Exhibition filled Ada with a new sense of hope. She was still only in her mid-thirties; there was plenty of time left for her to really make her mark. She thought that life couldn't get much better than that.

But Ada's own body had other ideas.

Terrible News

Just a few weeks after the Great Exhibition, Ada began to bleed for days at a time. The human body can't afford to lose too much blood, and whenever the bleeding stopped, **Ada felt drained and exhausted**.

Ada's doctor, Dr. Locock, was summoned, but she didn't want to make a fuss.

And so the treatments began:

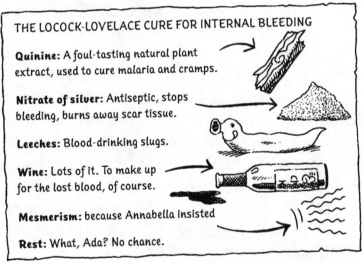

THE LOCOCK-LOVELACE CURE FOR INTERNAL BLEEDING

Quinine: A foul-tasting natural plant extract, used to cure malaria and cramps.

Nitrate of silver: Antiseptic, stops bleeding, burns away scar tissue.

Leeches: Blood-drinking slugs.

Wine: Lots of it. To make up for the lost blood, of course.

Mesmerism: because Annabella insisted

Rest: What, Ada? No chance.

But the doctor hadn't got the diagnosis quite right. There was certainly a growth, but it definitely wasn't healthy. **Ada had cancer**.

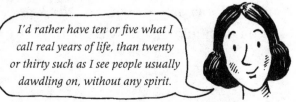

I'd rather have ten or five what I call real years of life, than twenty or thirty such as I see people usually dawdling on, without any spirit.

Once Ada realized she might not have much time left, she was determined to use every second she had. She now knew the Analytical Engine was not going to happen in her lifetime, but surely she could prove herself in some other way?

She wasn't really well enough to travel much, but she could still keep writing to Babbage and other scientists.

Dear Babs, I have an idea . . .

Sadly, Ada was suffering from cancer of the womb, and nineteenth-century medicine offered no treatment. As the pain grew worse and worse, Dr. Locock prescribed opium (another seriously dangerous painkiller) to help Ada cope. It dulled her mind so much that she couldn't think, and it was highly addictive.

Meanwhile, William made a fateful decision. Still reeling from the news about Ada's debts and now with his wife desperately ill, he needed someone to turn to and, unfortunately, he chose Annabella. **He told her everything.**

Mother Moves In

Annabella was aghast. OK, so Ada was seriously ill. She could handle that. It was the other stuff.

Addiction and gambling! So that's why she borrowed all that money.

It seemed Ada had turned out just like her father after all!

There was only one way to stop all this, Annabella decided: Ada needed her mother now more than ever. Slowly but surely, she wheedled her way into the family home until there was no getting rid of her.

Annabella wanted Ada off the opium, so she overrode the doctor's advice and called in a pair of mesmerists who waved their hands over Ada to no avail.

She also wasted no time in finding out all the facts about Ada's debts. When Anabella discovered that William had known about them all along, that was absolutely the final straw. William, she decided, was a totally unsuitable husband. From now on, **she would run Ada's life**. Dependent on Annabella for his income, William really couldn't argue.

Annabella didn't waste any time. First, she fired most of Ada's household servants and replaced them with her own. Then she fired Dr. Locock and brought in her personal doctor. At least he wasn't into mesmerism, but what he did prescribe was hardly going to help:

Effervescent ammonia —used as a toilet cleaner today!

POW!
Effervescent Ammonia

None of it made any difference. By the start of 1852, Ada was living with terrible pain and was confined to a wheelchair and the ground floor of their home. One small plus, however, was that her wheelchair was fitted with the latest technology . . .

I'll give you a push.

No thank you, Mother.

Can't get upstairs . . .

. . . but new rubber tires guarantee a nice, smooth ride.

Amazingly, in August 1852 Ada managed to pose for a final portrait by Henry Phillips, the son of Thomas Phillips, who had painted the famous curtain-covered portrait of her dad. He showed her sitting at a piano, fingers on the keys, but it was clear she was ill. Her eyes and cheeks were sunken. Her arms were like sticks. She was thin and wasted from the disease.

Phillips could have painted the picture in any colors he liked, but he made it look almost like a black-and-white photo. A photo of a person at the end of her life.

The end *was* **very near** for Ada, but she stayed positive. She kept on writing to Babbage and her other friends.

10   ADA'S LAST LAUGH

Charles Babbage came to visit Ada on August 12, 1852. He had stuck by her throughout her illness and all the difficult times. By now, Ada knew she was dying and she was making preparations. There was no one she trusted more than Babbage to do what she wanted—not even William.

So Ada gave Babbage a letter with instructions for after her death.

We don't know what the projects she mentions were, and as it turned out, Babbage couldn't carry out Ada's wishes, because the letter wasn't a proper will. Babbage could only follow Ada's instructions if

This is my will, Babbage:

Get money from my mother, to be spent on the projects we have discussed.

Get my bank to give you the balance currently in my account.

Take charge of all my property and papers, and do whatever you like with them.

A. A. L.

Annabella agreed. And did she? Absolutely not.

In fact, Annabella was so furious that Ada had trusted Babbage over her own mother that Babbage was **never allowed to see Ada again**. Ada was distraught. Her last link with her dearest friend had been cut and there was nothing she could do about it.

Annabella didn't stop there. The weaker Ada became, the more her mother cut her off from anyone else who could support her. She even persuaded William that if Ada had any chance at all, it was only through her own nonstop care. **He needed permission to visit his own wife** in his own home.

Ada's daughter, young Annabella, was allowed to help look after her mother. Young Byron, now sixteen, was summoned from his ship (he'd been in the Royal Navy for three years). However, Ralph, now thirteen, was at school in Switzerland. While Ada could send him speedy messages by telegraph, getting the boy back to London, to her bedside, took a lot longer.

Only people on Annabella's approved list got to see Ada: certain family members, doctors, some of Annabella's friends . . . and the Furies.

Get them out of here!

Ralph finally arrived on August 26, and Ada seemed better for having all her children at her side. She'd had her ups and downs with them in the past, but they really mattered to her.

Ada clung to life for another three months. Three long months of Annabella's fussing, and no friends allowed, until, finally, she died on November 27, 1852.

Annabella must have grieved for her, but maybe she also breathed a small sigh of satisfaction. She had had Ada under her control right until the end!

Or had she . . . ?

Poetry and Science Together

Ada gave William very precise instructions about how and where she wanted to be buried, and for once the law was in her favor. He was Ada's husband and he didn't have to ask for Annabella's permission. It turned out that, on their visit to Newstead two years earlier, **Ada had made a plan** and she'd got permission to be buried in the family vault of the local church.

Strangely, her father had been the same age as Ada when he died—just thirty-six—but thanks to the many developments in technology, the journey that Byron took to his final resting place was very different from the one that Ada took twenty-eight years later.

BYRON'S FUNERAL PROCESSION

- 📎 **Date:** July 1824
- 📎 **Method of transport:** horse-drawn hearse all the way from London
- 📎 **Time it took:** three days

ADA'S FUNERAL PROCESSION

- 📎 **Date:** December 1852
- 📎 **Method of transport:** Midland Railway Company most of the way; horse-drawn hearse from the station
- 📎 **Time it took:** a few hours

While all Ada's friends were there, the Furies weren't—Ada had to die to get rid of them completely! Just two family members didn't make it. Young Byron was stuck back on his ship, and **Annabella "stayed away."** By being buried at her father's home, Ada had finally slipped out of Annabella's control. She'd always refused to take Ada to Newstead, so to show up now would have been a total humiliation.

Ada's coffin was covered in violet velvet and studded with silver coronets and the Lovelace arms. On the lid was the Lovelace motto that seemed to fit the way Ada had lived her life.

Augusta Ada King-Noel
Countess of Lovelace
December 10, 1815–November 27, 1852
Labor ipse voluptas

Finally, Ada was laid to rest next to her father. She'd never known him, yet in the end she had felt closer to the man who had given her an imagination than to her mother, who had tried so hard to suppress it.

There's no record of how Annabella felt, but it would be nice to think that at some point she realized she should be proud for bringing up a daughter who had **the mind of a scientist and the imagination**

of a poet. Ada was a daughter both parents should have been proud of. A daughter who would not be forgotten.

AFTER ADA

Sadly, the Victorian computer age never happened. Difference Engine No. 2 and the Analytical Engine were never made—at least, not in Ada's or Babbage's lifetime. Babbage took up other causes, but he was tinkering with the design of the Analytical Engine until the day he died, in 1871, at age seventy-nine.

Over 100 years later, some engineers dug out the designs for Difference Engine No. 2 and there are now two fully working models of the machine, one in the Science Museum in London, and the other in Seattle. The machine works exactly as Babbage and Ada said it would.

The Analytical Engine never even got off the ground, unfortunately, but the idea didn't die.

And the *idea* of machines . . .

That can do things on their own.

That can think.

That can process information and create art and compose music . . .

All that came from Ada.

AND THERE'S MORE . . .

Ada lived in an age of clockwork and steam power. If only she'd made it to the ripe old age of eighty-nine, she might have witnessed the development that could make her ideas a reality:

1904—The invention of the vacuum tube finally made modern computers possible. It does the same thing in a computer as a wheel in the Analytical Engine, but much more quickly.

Wheel, used in Analytical Engine: makes things happen in a few seconds by turning.

Vacuum tube, used in early computers: makes things happen instantly by controlling electric current flow.

1930s and 40s—Modern computers really took off during and after World War II. Computer science was invented at this time, and technicians began to understand concepts like programming, processing, and memory.

Colossus Mark 2: one of the computers that helped the Allies win World War II.

Take that, Hitler!

1940s and 1950s—Vacuum tubes were replaced by transistors. Computers got smaller and faster. Computer scientists worked out that if you're processing numbers, you can process anything. Just as Ada had predicted.

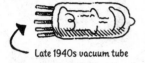

Late 1940s vacuum tube

Early 1950s transistor

1953—Ada's Notes were rediscovered and republished. All those modern computer scientists were shocked to discover that their ideas weren't new after all. Someone had got there 100 years before them—and that someone was a woman. Ada finally began to get the fame she deserved.

1960s—Silicon chips started to replace transistors. Computers got even smaller and even faster.

Unbelievable!

Mid-1950s transistor

Modern silicon chip: contains literally hundreds of millions of transistors

1970s—The American government started developing its own computer language for all its projects. They named it Ada in Countess Lovelace's honor, and even included her birth year in the specification number: MIL-STD-1815. Today Ada is the language used by air traffic control systems around the world, so you could say that Ada finally did get to fly!

They've developed flyology!

ADA REFERENCE MANUAL

1980s—Commands started to be made using pictures (or graphical interfaces) rather than text.

Well, of course!

1990s–2000s—Next, came handheld digital devices . . .

Music, text, and pictures reduced to numbers in a machine's memory—just as I knew they could be.

1998—The British Computer Society released the Lovelace Medal, given to "individuals who have made an outstanding contribution to the understanding or advancement of Computing." The 2018 winner was Professor Gordon Plotkin, for his work on computer programming languages

2009—The first Ada Lovelace Day was celebrated, "to raise the profile of women in science, technology, engineering, and math." Ada was never taken quite as seriously as male mathematicians of her day. Now, Ada Lovelace Day is celebrated the second Tuesday of every October.

Yesss!

Ada's life was far too short, and while she lived, acknowledgement of her work and her genius was almost nonexistent. Perhaps if she'd been a man then people would have listened more carefully to her very original ideas.

Today, though, her name is known worldwide and her amazing achievements are rightfully recognized. Despite prejudice against her, and despite her physical and mental illness, she fought on through and planted the ideas that **made computer science possible**.

Ideas survive even if people die. Look around you: how much of what you can see depends on computers?

That's Ada's legacy. Over 160 years so far, and counting.

TIMELINE

So little time . . .
yet so much achieved!

1815
George Gordon Byron
(Lord Byron) and Anne
Isabella Milbanke marry.

December 10, 1815
Augusta Ada Byron (a.k.a. Ada
Lovelace) is born.

| 1815 | 1820

1816
Baby Ada is "stolen" by
Annabella, and Lord Byron
flees to Europe.

1824
Lord Byron dies.

1829
Ada gets the measles—and doesn't recover for three years!

| 1825

| 1830

1833
At age seventeen, Ada is presented to the king and officially becomes a young lady.

Ada meets Charles Babbage and is entranced by his Difference Engine.

1828
Ada develops "flyology."

1835
Ada meets and marries
Lord William King.

Ada places her first bet.

1836
Ada's first son,
Byron, is born.

| 1830

| 1835

1837
Ada's daughter, Annabella,
is born.

Ada catches cholera.

1838
Ada becomes Lady
Augusta Ada King-Noel,
Countess of Lovelace.

1842

Luigi Federico Menabrea publishes an article about the Analytical Engine in French.

Ada translates the article and adds her own Notes at the end.

1839

Ada's second son, Ralph, is born.

| 1840

| 1845

1843

Ada writes to Charles Babbage offering to become his project manager for the Analytical Engine. He refuses.

Ada's translation of Menabrea's article with her Notes is published.

SKETCH
OF THE
ANALYTICAL ENGINE
INVENTED BY
CHARLES BABBAGE, Esq.
BY L. F. MENABREA,
of Turin,
OFFICER OF THE MILITARY ENGINEERS.
WITH NOTES BY THE TRANSLATOR.
[Extracted from the "SCIENTIFIC MEMOIRS," vol.III]

• 1848
Ada gets sick again.

• 1845
Ada works on her Calculus of the Nervous System.

| 1845

| 1850

• 1850
Ada and William visit Newstead Abbey, where Byron lived. Ada feels a connection with her father.

• 1851
Ada loses thousands of pounds betting on horses at the Derby.

Ada and William visit the Great Exhibition in London.

Ada develops cancer.

1852

Annabella bans Ada and Charles Babbage from seeing each other after Ada tries to give Babbage all her money and property.

November 27, 1852

Ada dies.

| 1855 | 1955

1953

Ada's Notes are rediscovered and republished, and finally she begins to get the recognition she deserves!

GLOSSARY

agriculture: Farming, that includes growing crops and breeding animals for food, wool, and other products.

algebraic: Related to algebra (math where letters and other symbols represent numbers).

$$\frac{x}{e^x-1} = \sum_{n=0}^{\infty} \frac{B_n x^n}{n!}$$

analytical: Involving detailed examination and investigation of something.

ancestor: a person from an earlier generation of the same family, or an earlier model of a machine.

antiseptic: Something that stops the spread of germs which cause disease.

aristocratic: Being part of a noble family in a high social position.

atom: The very smallest building block of every material that exists.

British Empire: A large group of countries that used to be ruled by the United Kingdom, including India, Canada, and Australia.

calculus: A branch of math that finds patterns between similar sums and uses formulas to help understanding.

chemistry: A type of science that studies the properties of different substances—what they're made up of, why they behave the way they do, and what happens when you combine them.

computer software: Programs and operating systems that tell a computer how to perform a task.

cube: To multiply a number by itself three times (for example, $2 \times 2 \times 2 = 8$, which can be written as: $2^3 = 8$).

electric current : A flow of electric energy.

eligible: Allowed to participate in an activity.

engineering: Designing and making complicated products using math and science.

equation: A sum where both sides of the equals sign have the same value, e.g., $\frac{1}{2} = \frac{2}{4}$ or $1 + 5 = 3 + 3$

formula: A mathematic or scientific rule or statement, written using letters and symbols.

hardware: The physical parts of a computer system.

hearse: A carriage that takes a coffin (and the body inside it) to a funeral or burial site.

intellect: The ability to reason and understand.

legacy: Money, property, a reputation, or ideas that are passed down as part of your history, or remaining from an earlier time.

$1674 \div \frac{14}{7} \times 389{,}217 \div 0.000042$

logical: Based on clear reasoning.

manufacturer: Someone who makes products, usually by machine, but sometimes by hand.

menagerie: A collection of animals, usually wild or exotic.

molecule: A tiny unit of a substance, made of a group of two or more atoms.

nervous system: The network of nerves in the human body, and most animals—made up of the brain, spinal cord, nerves, and sense organs like eyes and ears—which controls how the body works.

new-fangled: The newest style—often very different from what is normal or expected.

oscillating: Swinging steadily back and forth.

physics: A type of science that studies matter, forces and their effects with the aim of understanding how the universe behaves.

pulley: A simple machine using a grooved wheel and cord that makes lifting an object easier.

rank : Position in society.

shilling: A coin used in England from the 1500s to 1970—20 shillings made up one pound.

solitaire: A game for one person played with pegs on a board.

spouse: Husband or wife; partner in marriage.

statics: A branch of math that studies objects or bodies at rest.

status: Position in relation to other people in society.

suitor: A man who seeks a relationship with a particular woman with the aim of marrying her.

textiles: Cloths and fabrics.

tinkerer: Somebody who repairs and experiments (or tinkers) with machines.

vaccination: An injection that helps the body to prevent a particular infection.

vault: A chamber in a church or graveyard where bodies are buried.

vengeance: Punishing, or taking revenge on someone, for having wronged someone else.

visionary: Someone who uses imagination and wisdom to think about the future.

I never am really satisfied that I understand anything.

NOTES

7   "I awoke . . . famous": Thomas Moore, *Letters and Journals of Lord Byron*. London: J. Murray, 1830; page 159.

34   "Every moment . . . is born": Alfred, Lord Tennyson, "The Vision of Sin" in "Tennyson's poems: The Vision of Sin." *GradeSaver*. See www.gradesaver.com/tennysons-poems/e-text/the-vision-of-sin.

34   "I believe . . . poetry": Doron Swade, *The Difference Engine*. New York: Penguin Books, 2002; page 77.

42   "Whatever number . . . difference": Charles Babbage, *The Life of a Philosopher*. Cambridge: Cambridge University Press, 2011; page 65.

73   "It demonstrates . . . anticipate": Benjamin Woolley, *The Bride of Science*. New York: McGraw-Hill, 2000; page 267.

74   "The Analytical Engine . . . and leaves": Betty A. Toole, *Ada, the Enchantress of Numbers*. Moreton-in-Marsh, UK: Strawberry Press, 1998; page 182.

80   "I would . . . at you!": Toole, *Ada, the Enchantress of Numbers*, page 154.

81   "She is . . . exerted": Sydney Padua, *The Thrilling Adventures of Lovelace and Babbage*. New York: Pantheon, 2015; pages 274–275.

91   "Unfortunately . . . nothing more": Toole, *Ada, the Enchantress of Numbers*, page 230.

93   "I shall . . . brain": Toole, *Ada, the Enchantress of Numbers*, page 214.

101 "produce . . . somethings": Woolley, *The Bride of Science*, page 340.

117 "I'd rather . . . any spirit": Woolley, *The Bridge of Science*, page 344.

139 "I never . . . understand anything": "Quotations by Ada Lovelace." Strange Wondrous Quotes and Quotations. See strangewondrous.net/browse/author/l/lovelace+ada.

SELECT BIBLIOGRAPHY

Babbage, Charles. *The Life of a Philospher*. Cambridge, UK: Cambridge University Press, 2011.

Moore, Thomas. *Letters and Journals of Lord Byron*. London: J. Murray, 1830.

Padua, Sydney. *The Thrilling Adventures of Lovelace and Babbage: The (Mostly) True Story of the First Computer*. New York: Pantheon, 2015.

Swade, Doron. *The Difference Engine: Charles Babbage and the Quest to Build the First Computer*. New York: Penguin Books, 2002.

Tennyson, Alfred, Lord. "The Vision of Sin." Quoted in "Tennyson's Poems: The Vision of Sin." *GradeSaver*. See www.gradesaver.com/ tennysons-poems/e-text/the-vision-of-sin.

Toole, Betty A. *Ada, the Enchantress of Numbers: Prophet of the Computer Age*. Moreton-in-Marsh, UK: Strawberry Press, 1998.

Woolley, Benjamin. *The Bride of Science: Romance, Reason, and Byron's Daughter*. New York: McGraw-Hill, 2000.

INDEX

> Use these pages for a quick reference!

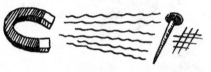

That's quite enough book learning for now.

Yes, be off with you!

About the Author

Ben Jeapes is a children's book author who also runs his own independent science fiction publishing house based in Abingdon, Oxfordshire.

About the Illustrator

Nick Ward is an illustrator, a writer, and the creator of several popular picture books for children. He lives in England.

GET TO KNOW ANOTHER
FASCINATING FIGURE
IN THE NEXT BOOK IN THE

THE FIRST
NAMES SERIES

"Don't tell me I can't go to school!"

Lisa Williamson ★ Illustrated by Mike Smith

Introduction

October 9, 2012
Mingora, Swat Valley, Pakistan

Malala was in a good mood traveling home from school. She was pretty sure she'd aced the test that morning and was looking forward to a relaxing afternoon at home.

She was laughing with her best friend, Moniba, when **the school bus stopped suddenly**. A young man was standing in the road. He wore long white robes and a baseball cap.

"Is this the Khushal School bus?" he asked.

Another young man jumped onto the back of the bus. A hush fell over the girls as both men glared at them. Heart hammering in her chest, Malala found Moniba's hand and gave it a squeeze. Around twenty girls were crammed onto the hard plastic benches and they stared back, stunned, as the men scanned the bus.

"Who is Malala?" the second man asked gruffly. No one answered, but a few of the girls glanced in Malala's direction before they could stop themselves. Then the same man **raised a pistol**.

Malala froze with fear.

The man fixed his gaze on her and aimed his pistol at her head. The other girls began to scream, but Malala didn't make a sound. She just squeezed Moniba's hand harder.

A split second later, the man pulled the trigger and **everything went black**.

Malala was bleeding pro-fusely as the bus swerved through the heaving streets of Mingora, speeding toward the local hospital. Once there, doctors said her prospects were grim, so grim that with a heavy heart, Malala's dad **began making funeral arrangements**. For a short while it looked like the men had succeeded in their quest to silence her.

But Malala did not die; she survived, and within days of her shooting she had become one of most famous teenagers on the planet. And she was more determined than ever to stand up for what she believed in: that every single girl in the world deserved to go to school. And she wanted as many people to hear her message as possible. She has since written books, appeared on television, and met all sorts of important people, including President Obama and the Queen of England. She's also the youngest person ever to win the Nobel Peace Prize.

Incredible stuff, right?

> Yes, but I'm actually quite ordinary, you know.

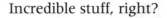

Yeah, right! Didn't Beyoncé wish you a happy birthday once?

> Well, yes . . .

And Selena Gomez called you her "role model!"

> OK, OK, but I promise you the real Malala isn't all that different from other girls.

Really?

> Yes! I love television, and I argue with my brothers over stupid things, like the TV remote and who ate the last slice of pizza!

You like pizza?

> Oh yes! And curry. And cupcakes. Mmmmm, especially cupcakes . . . And I like reading and listening to music and shopping and hanging out with my friends. Oh, and I hate getting up in the morning!

Hmm, all of that does sound pretty ordinary, actually.

So what makes Malala's story so special? Well, it didn't start with the shooting and the sudden fame. This ordinary girl was destined to achieve **extraordinary things** from the very moment she was born.

1 No Party for Malala

Ziauddin Yousafzai was over the moon. On the hot sticky morning of July 12, 1997 his wife gave birth to their first child—a beautiful bouncing baby girl. Over the next few days, he was so excited that he told everyone he met about the new addition to his family. People were polite but confused.

Why was he so happy and proud? After all, his wife had **a baby girl**. The thing is, in Pakistan, even today, from the second they enter the world, boys and girls are mostly treated very differently. When a baby boy is born, the family celebrates. Guns are fired up into the sky and visitors come to coo over the cradle and cram it with sweets and money. But when a baby girl is born . . . no gunshots, no gifts—people don't even bother to visit! Instead they sympathize with the "poor" mother and hope, for her sake, that her next child will be a boy.

Girls play as important a role in Pakistan as they do anywhere else in the world, but some families see raising girls as **a financial burden**. Girls aren't allowed to go out to work and provide for their families like boys do, and it can cost over a million rupees (about $15,000) to marry a daughter off.

Most girls spend their lives at home being wives and mothers, cooking and looking after the house and their children. And for some reason, that doesn't seem as important as earning a regular income. This is the way it's been for hundreds of years, which is why Ziauddin's celebrating his daughter was so unusual.

That's my dad for you! With a different set of parents, I'd probably be married with at least two babies by now.

To get to know me, you need to understand them first . . .

HIGH-FLYING ZIAUDDIN

Ziauddin had a habit of challenging tradition that started when he was a boy—**and brother to five sisters**! While he and his older brother went off to school, the girls stayed at home and learned how to run a house, so that when they got married and had families of their own, they'd know what to do. Ziauddin thought this seemed **really unfair**, and as soon as he was old enough, he planned to do something about it.

> But my dad had a really bad stutter, which made speaking in public unbelievably scary.

In spite of his stutter, Ziauddin entered a public speaking competition. He practiced and practiced and practiced until he knew his speech so well he could recite it in his sleep.

When the day of the competition rolled around, Ziauddin was terrified.

> A-hem . . .

Read on in the next title in the
FIRST NAMES series:
MALALA YOUSAFZAI